NEW HAMPSHIRE'S
KANCAMAGUS HIGHWAY

NEW HAMPSHIRE'S
KANCAMAGUS HIGHWAY

A History and Guide

GLENN A. KNOBLOCK

THE
History
PRESS

Published by The History Press
Charleston, SC
www.historypress.com

Copyright © 2022 by Glenn A. Knoblock
All rights reserved

First published 2022

Manufactured in the United States

ISBN 9781467152112

Library of Congress Control Number: 2022936205

CONTENTS

Acknowledgements   7
Introduction   9

PART I: THE HISTORY OF THE KANCAMAGUS ROUTE
1. The Native American Presence   13
2. The Settling of Conway, Albany and the
    Swift River Intervale   22
3. The Logging Railroads Stake Their Claim   32
4. The Beginnings of the White Mountain National Forest
    and the Kancamagus Highway   39
5. The Completion of the Kancamagus Highway and the Influence
    of Loon Mountain   45

PART II: A GUIDE TO DRIVING THE KANCAMAGUS HIGHWAY
6. Scenic Attractions along the Kanc   59
7. Trees and Wildlife along the Kanc   105
8. Camping along the Kanc   121
9. Hiking along the Kanc   127
10. More to Know Before You Go   142

Source Bibliography and Further Reading   153

Acknowledgements

As is always the case when writing a history book or guidebook, no author can undertake such a work without some expert help. I have been lucky to have the following individuals provide meaningful assistance.

David Govatski of Jefferson, New Hampshire, is a forester and environmental consultant with over thirty years of experience with the U.S. Forest Service. David is also active with the Forest History Society and was instrumental in providing the vintage images of the Kancamagus Highway.

Sarah Jordan is the heritage program manager and forest archaeologist for the U.S. Forest Service, White Mountain National Forest. She kindly answered my questions about the C.L. Graham Wangan Overlook and provided historic data.

Joseph M. Phillips is the visitor information supervisor and conservation education coordinator with the U.S. Forest Service, White Mountain National Forest at the Saco River Ranger Station. He kindly answered my questions during an impromptu visit and provided some of his own information about the Kancamagus Highway and its visitors.

Colleen Eliason is the communication and sales coordinator for the White Mountains Attractions Association (WMAA), located on the Kancamagus Highway in North Woodstock. She kindly answered my queries and gave permission to use the WMAA's tourist map of the highway in this book.

Rebecca Coleman of Wolfeboro, New Hampshire, a good friend, soon-to-be wife and avid hiker who's out on a trail every weekend (every day if she could!). She kindly provided her photos of Champney Falls and Pitcher Falls for inclusion here.

Jonny Lovering of Wolfeboro, New Hampshire, a friend, soon-to-be husband and avid hiker. He kindly reviewed the hiking chapter in this book.

Tina Marconi of Wolfeboro, a friend and accomplished hiker. Tina has not only climbed each of the four-thousand-footers but is now on her second go-around, hiking each of them in the winter season. She is also "redlining" the White Mountains, about 75 percent complete, hiking well over one thousand miles in the process. She patiently reviewed the hiking chapter and offered some "sweet" insights. Who knew there were "zombies" in the White Mountains!

John Compton, aka the Happy Hiker, of Bethlehem, New Hampshire. He kindly allowed for the use of his Church Pond photo. Check out his many White Mountain hikes at https://1happyhiker.blogspot.com/ for great commentary and more excellent photos.

Daniel Brausuell, for allowing the use of his GoPro photo from his whitewater kayaking adventure down the Swift River.

In addition to the above contributors, I'd also like to thank my editor, Mike Kinsella. This is a book he suggested, and it is our third collaboration together. Mike, too, has had his experiences on the Kanc, so he knows whereof he edits, so to speak. Despite all this help, any errors that remain are strictly my doing.

Finally, great thanks go to my wife, Terry Knoblock. Not only is she my biggest supporter on whatever book project I'm working on, but she also provides valuable editorial advice (even if we don't always agree!). For this book, she traveled up and down the Kanc with me numerous times, offering manuscript tweaks and photo suggestions and also, equally importantly, as a companion traveler! This book wouldn't have been nearly as fun to write and photograph without her. Terry has, in fact, been my traveling companion on life's highway for over forty years now. I wouldn't trade any of it for the world, and I know we've got much more to see and experience and, hopefully, many more miles to log.

—Glenn A. Knoblock
Wolfeboro Falls, New Hampshire
March 2022

Introduction

Kancamagus. The very name invokes the mystery and majesty of New Hampshire's White Mountains, but how did this come to be the name of one of New England's most scenic highways? Relatively few people outside New Hampshire know the origins of the highway and the name it bears, even though over one million people travel the highway every year, and many can neither pronounce nor spell its name correctly. For the record, the correct pronunciation is *Kank*-a-ma-gus, but many locals just call it the "Kanc."

Now that that matter is settled, what about the highway itself? As highways and byways go, at first glance its history would seem to be a rather short one; the highway was completed in 1959, but it was not open for year-round travel until 1967. Since that time, it has evolved into the road we travel today to take in its scenic splendor. However, the history of the land through which the Kancamagus Highway passes, and of the people who inhabited the region long before the automobile was invented, is a much longer account. This byway actually took over one hundred years to be developed into the highway we know today, and even before that time, the area it traverses was a highway of sorts, first for Native American peoples and later for the first settlers of European ancestry. By understanding this interesting history, we come to understand the full significance of the Kancamagus Highway.

I first traveled the Kancamagus Highway nearly forty years ago. My wife and I were young then, and we made the trip, east to west, in her 1979 Chevy Chevette, whose small engine had the power of a sewing machine. It was an exciting ride, especially climbing Kancamagus Pass (where the car labored mightily) and going around the hairpin turn for the first time (the brakes were in poor shape). And all the while, we took in the beautiful mountain scenery. I have since that time traveled the Kanc, both for business and pleasure, more times than I can count, including many times during the period in which this book was being researched and written. If there's one thing that I've learned about the Kancamagus Highway over the years, it's the fact that driving the route just once, or twice (once in each direction), is not enough to truly know it. Until you've driven the Kancamagus Highway in all the seasons of the year and at varying times of both the day and nighttime hours and stopped to experience its natural attractions along the way, you haven't truly experienced the splendors of this short but magnificent highway and all it has to offer. Over nearly four decades of travel, I've seen sights that I hadn't seen or noticed before nearly every time I make the trip, and there are some things I've yet to see: a moose along the highway or, better yet, crossing it, is top of my list. But no matter; I'm lucky enough to live close by. For those of you who don't have the opportunity to travel the Kanc regularly, perhaps because you come from afar, and want to learn more about the journey you've just made, or are soon to make, this book is for you. However, it's also for those of you who, like myself, live nearby and perhaps take the Kanc for granted or don't know the full story of its history. Either way, it will remind you of why you've come to drive the Kancamagus Highway, whether for the first time or the hundredth time. Enjoy!

PART I

THE HISTORY OF THE KANCAMAGUS ROUTE

Chapter 1

THE NATIVE AMERICAN PRESENCE

The Kancamagus Highway is 34.5 miles long, running from Conway in eastern New Hampshire west to Lincoln in central New Hampshire. Except for these two population centers, most of the highway runs through an area that, but for a few seasonal residents, is largely unpopulated year-round. That is one of the allures of the highway: the quick and distinctive change from driving through built-up and developed areas to, within a few short miles, driving on a wilderness road that passes through a scenic mountain landscape. Except for those cars on the highway itself, the land around it appears wild, untamed and even, at some times of the year, desolate. However, that has not been the case for much of the highway route's history, during which time humans have inhabited the area for thousands of years, living in settlements that at times numbered close to 1,500 people, perhaps more.

The first settlers known to have been here may have been the peoples of the so-called Clovis culture who, it is speculated, first migrated to North America via the land bridge that once crossed the Bering Strait between Siberia and Alaska. These peoples, known as Paleo-Indians for the distinctive type of stone tools they fashioned, arrived here approximately eleven thousand years ago, possibly longer. Archaeologist Richard Boisvert, who was New Hampshire's state archaeologist for over thirty years, has written of their presence in New Hampshire that "the Paleoindians were the first people to enter the landscape and they must be recognized as pioneers in the strictest sense of the word." As he has documented in his research and

An aerial panoramic view of the west end of the Kancamagus Highway. The hairpin turn is at left. *Wangkun Jia, Shutterstock.*

writings, Paleo-Indian artifacts and sites have been discovered at various places in the White Mountains, including at Intervale in North Conway and the Israel River Complex in Jefferson. The area along the Swift River, which is paralleled by the Kancamagus Highway for much of its length, has also been the site of artifact discoveries, especially in the Swift River Intervale (also known as Passaconaway). The Paleo-Indians, about whom little is known, were migratory hunters, constantly on the move in search of the big caribou that provided them with both food and hides that they used for clothing. While the reasons for their eventual demise are far from certain—perhaps over-hunting or the advent of another ice age—the Paleo-Indians are considered the ancestors of all later Indigenous peoples. Indeed, it's not hard to imagine these hunters at work along the area of the Kancamagus, stalking their prey and making a successful kill, perhaps around Sawyer or Lily Pond or near one of the many mountain streams that flow through the area.

While we don't know much about the Paleo-Indians, we have a better idea of the Native American peoples that were living along the Kancamagus route when European settlers first arrived here in the early 1600s. The predominant group in the area was the Pequawket Tribe (also known as "Pigwacket" and many other spelling variants). They were part of a larger ethnic group, the Abenaki Nation, that speaks the Algonquin language and was predominant in much of what is now New Hampshire and Maine

when European settlers first arrived here early in the 1600s. Not only has archaeological evidence been found of their presence along the Swift River, but Irish immigrant Darby Field also journeyed by water up the coast from Dover, New Hampshire, led by Native American guides, and thence up the Saco River in birchbark canoes. It was at modern-day Fryeburg that he encountered the main settlement of the Pequawket Tribe before journeying farther north to make the first ascent of what is now known as Mount Washington, the first European to do so. This event took place in either 1632 or 1642, but which year this event took place, surviving accounts do not make clear.

The Native Americans of New Hampshire lived off the land, hunting, fishing and gathering wild roots, berries and bark but also growing crops to provide for their needs. These were primarily beans, winter squash and maize (corn), collectively known as the Three Sisters. However, it is likely that in the White Mountain region, the growing season was too short for maize, unlike the more moderate conditions found in southern New Hampshire. Later on, when white settlers moved into the Swift River Intervale, they, too, would find good land for farming—it was one of the few places where the soil was not too rocky and barren—and an outstanding source for fish. As to the wild animals found along the Kancamagus Highway, the moose, bear and deer that offer travelers today a thrilling glimpse of nature in northern New Hampshire were, in this earlier age, vital staples in the life of Native Americans. Their meat provided food, and their hides were used for clothing and shelter. Other parts, like bone, antler and sinew, were used to make tools; nothing went to waste.

Features of the geography on the southern side of the Kancamagus Highway in the Sandwich Range, fittingly, bear the names of some of the most legendary of the leaders among these Native peoples. The Passaconaway area of Albany and Mount Passaconaway (4,043 ft.) are named after the noted sachem of the Penacook Tribe, which lived along the Merrimack River in southern New Hampshire, with major villages at modern-day Nashua, Concord and Lowell, Massachusetts. Passaconaway, who was born sometime between 1550 and 1570, was a prominent warrior in his younger days who fought against their enemy, the Mohawk Tribe, which often made incursions into New England from the west to threaten the Penacooks. By the time the first white settlers arrived in New Hampshire, Passaconaway was a *bashaba* (chief of chiefs), the head of a federation of a number of Abenaki tribes located throughout Massachusetts and northern New England. Passaconaway never lived in the area along the Kancamagus Highway, his primary home being at Pawtucket Falls in what is now Lowell, Massachusetts. However, he did hold sway over the tribes there, including the Pequawket. Known as a powerful shaman among his own people and also highly regarded by the English for his supernatural powers, Passaconaway is said by historian and Native American scholar Mary Ellen Lepionka to have gone "on retreat into the White Mountains for months at a time to work at getting rid of the Europeans by casting spells, coming out periodically to see if they were working." The fact that they did not, she speculates, may have led to his abdication. Passaconaway was noted for getting along with the English settlers, even if the alliance was a difficult one, and was one of the first of the Native American chiefs in New England willing to sell land to them. After having ruled for decades, Passaconaway abdicated his position about 1660 and designated his son as his successor. In his farewell address to his people, he asked that his people always remain at peace with the English. The aged chief is thought to have died by 1669.

Artist's rendition of Chief Passaconaway, a *bashaba* of the Penacook Tribe. *From C.E. Potter's History of Manchester, New Hampshire, 1856.*

Mount Wonalancet (2,760 ft.) is named after the son of Passaconaway. Wonalancet would continue in his father's footsteps in trying to remain allied with the English and even kept his confederation of tribes out of King Philip's War (1675–78), a last-ditch effort by Native Americans in southern New England to stop the English from taking their land. The time of his leadership was marked by a further decline in the Native American presence in New Hampshire and New England as a whole. Despite remaining friendly to the English, Wonalancet's own people, the Penacooks, continued to be pushed off their land by English settlers, and many were killed or sold into slavery in the Caribbean, including members of Wonalancet's own family. In 1675, the Penacook village at what is now Concord was attacked by the English and burned to the ground without provocation, with survivors fleeing northward to the White Mountains, where Wonalancet had gone, for their own safety and survival. The following year, the *bashaba* returned south to Cocheco (Dover, New Hampshire) to meet with the colonial leader, Captain Richard Waldron. The delegation led by Wonalancet included several hundred tribal leaders from the confederation of tribes ruled by him. However, in an act of treachery that would not be forgotten, the delegation was captured by Waldron and his men by deceitful means, with some subsequently executed and many of them sent into slavery to the south. Others, including Wonalancet, were eventually released; Wonalancet returned to Penacook lands in northern New Hampshire. By 1685, he had abdicated his position, but in his old age returned to the area of his birth in 1692. He was quickly arrested and placed in home confinement, dying in 1697 in the area of Lowell, Massachusetts, on the island where he had been born.

The Kancamagus Highway itself, along with Mount Kancamagus (3,762 ft.) and Kancamagus Pass, are named after Wonalancet's successor as *bashaba* of the Penacook Confederation. Kancamagus, whose name means Fearless One, was the grandson of Passaconaway and the nephew of Wonalancet. Little is known of his life, except for the fact that he lived up to his name and was the last Penacook leader of the Native American confederacy. Having seen the treachery of the English settlers, despite the peaceful policies of his grandfather and uncle, Kancamagus was determined to fight for his people. Kancamagus, who could speak and write English and was called John Hawkins by the colonial officials, first tried to get along with New Hampshire's royal government and advocated for his people's rights, but he was largely ignored by royal government officials. When the English allied themselves with the Mohawks, the longtime enemy of the Penacooks, this led Kancamagus to establish an alliance with the French in Canada (England's main rival in North America at the time) and take the fight to the English settlers who were taking his people's lives and land. In June 1689, he led a raid against the settlement at Dover, New Hampshire, specifically targeting the home of Major Richard Waldron, who had acted treacherously against Wonalancet over a decade before. Five garrison houses of the settlement, which had a population of about two hundred, were attacked in the early morning hours. The main target was Waldron himself, who after a fierce fight was captured in his own home and tortured before being killed. Many of the warriors who took part in this raid had family members who were sold into slavery or killed by the English. When Waldron was tied to a chair in his own home, a number of warriors took their knives and slashed his body, each one calling out "I cross out my account" after doing so. In all, twenty-three settlers were killed, while twenty-six more were taken to Canada and sold, some of these captives later being redeemed and returning home. It was a shocking raid to the early New Hampshire settlers, but it was not as wanton as some early writers and historians have suggested. Indeed, some in Dover were spared because the warriors had known they were not part of Waldron's earlier treachery and were known for their kind treatment of Native Americans. Despite the raid by Kancamagus, the writing was on the wall for him and the Penacooks. He continued the fight for several more years, but in 1691 he accepted defeat and signed a peace treaty. He moved his people northward, first to the White Mountains and then to St. Francis, a Native American village in Quebec founded by French Jesuit missionaries. With such a move, the Native American presence in New Hampshire was greatly reduced, and while some individuals remained, the Penacooks were no longer an organized entity in their homeland. What became of Kancamagus and details of his life and death after his removal to Canada are lost to history. It is quite possible, though far from certain, that he later led attacks against the English from St. Francis. He thus remains a shadowy and somewhat mysterious figure in New Hampshire history, and so it is appropriate that he eventually came to be honored in the naming of the Kancamagus Highway. Even today, relatively few people know about this fierce leader who waged a battle to save his people. Interestingly, I lived in Dover for many years, just a short distance from the site of Richard Waldron's homestead. Little did I realize back then that in traveling from Dover on a fall weekend to take a ride along the Kanc, I was traveling roughly the same route that Kancamagus had traveled nearly three centuries before. Reflecting on this now, I realize that from that time to this, the White Mountains have provided a place of respite and refuge for the people of New Hampshire and beyond through all the ages. Traveling there in our age offers a chance to get back to nature, to get away from it all, if even for a brief time. Kancamagus and his people, too, sought refuge there but, sadly, with the knowledge that they could never again return to their homes.

Two other mountains along the route of the Kancamagus Highway are also named after Native Americans with a connection to the White Mountains. Mount Paugus (3,198 ft.) is named after a man who was, by legend, said to have been a famed sachem of the Pequawket Tribe. He was killed in a battle known to most New Englanders as Lovewell's Fight, also called the Battle of Pequawket. This took place at the site of Fryeburg, Maine, on May 9, 1725, and was the last battle in a running conflict between the English and the French and their allies, the tribes of the Wabanaki Confederacy (mostly from Maine), known as Governor Dummer's War (1722–25). Native Americans from Canada and Maine had made incursions as far south as Massachusetts, including at Dunstable (now Nashua, New Hampshire) in the fall of 1724, killing a number of people. Captain John Lovewell of that town formed his own raiding party to counter these attacks, and with the incentive of the bounties for Native American scalps offered by the Massachusetts government, he traveled north with his men to Maine to take his fight to the Native peoples and collect scalps. His third expedition northward culminated in Lovewell's Fight, when his force, consisting of thirty-four men (ten others were left behind to man a makeshift fort at Ossipee), encountered an Abenaki raiding party along the banks of what is now known as Lovewell's Pond in modern-day Fryeburg, Maine. In the ensuing firefight, Lovewell was killed, as were twelve other men. The losses among the Native Americans are unknown for certain but much smaller in number. One man known to have been killed is Paugus, who was asserted by tradition to have been a chief of the Pequawkets. This is actually inaccurate, as are the legends surrounding his life details and death. In fact, Paugus—whose real name was likely Paucanaulemet, according to historian Fannie Hardy Eckstorm—was a member of the Schaghticoke Tribe of western Connecticut who was previously captured by the Mohawks. While a ward of that tribe, he was hunting around Concord, New Hampshire, when he was captured by the English and kept imprisoned at Boston for over a year. He was eventually released at the request of the Mohawks and, after his release, made his way to St. Francis in Quebec, where he allied himself with the French.

From St. Francis, he led raids down through Maine and New Hampshire into Massachusetts, including the raid against Dunstable in the fall of 1724. He would lead further raids in Maine until his death in the Battle of Pequawket on May 9, 1725. Following this battle, most of the members of the Pequawket Tribe, even those who had tried to remain on good terms with the English, saw what was coming and removed northward to Canada, where they were protected by the French.

Finally, Mount Chocorua (3,480 ft.) is also said to have been named after a chief of the Pequawket Tribe. While there are several versions of the legend, the common threads are that Chocorua had a young son who either stayed with the Campbell family in what is now Tamworth or wandered from his father's home to their home. While there, he ingested a poison used to kill foxes and died while Chocorua was away, or he came home and died later from being poisoned. Either way, the chief blamed the Campbells and subsequently killed several members of the family. For this deed, he was pursued by a group of local men, making his way to the top of the mountain that now bears his name. In one version, it is said he leaped to his death from the summit rather than be captured, while in another version, he was shot by Mr. Campbell. Either way, before his death he laid a curse upon the land in the area around the mountain and the white men who lived there, and for the next one hundred years, the cattle in the area were afflicted and died, said to be a result of Chocorua's curse. While the story is an interesting one and has been passed down by New England writers since the 1820s, historian Mary Ellen Lepionka makes the case that it is apocryphal in nature. She states that such curses were an "Anglo-European invention and literary genre" and further makes the case that while "Native curses traditionally invoked spiritual interventions," they did not give natural features of the landscape, like the land itself or mountains, the power to "effect curses." Furthermore, there is no known sachem of the Pequawkets who was named Chocorua, and while the legends behind the name may be broadly based on a Native American of the past whose identity has not been otherwise preserved, as well as interactions between members of the tribe and early white settlers, Lepionka's studies indicate that the mountain was probably not named after a person at all. Indeed, this was not the custom of the Algonquian peoples, and it is more likely that the mountain's name translates to Home of the Water Serpent, based on Native customs and religious beliefs. Though it is impossible at this late date to know the true story behind the mysterious name of Mount Chocorua, both the legend and the historical possibilities are a fascinating part of the lore of the White Mountains.

With the further defeats of Native American bands and incursions northward by English explorers and settlers into what was once their territory in the 1720s, along with the removal of the surviving tribes to Canada, the Native American presence in New Hampshire was largely ended, though some individuals and families in very small numbers did remain. A new chapter in the history of the region would soon follow.

Chapter 2

THE SETTLING OF CONWAY, ALBANY
AND THE SWIFT RIVER INTERVALE

The beginnings of the Kancamagus Highway would come from the east. With the removal of the Native American tribes, the area of the White Mountains would remain unsettled from the 1730s until after the end of the wars that took place in northern New England, including King George's War (1744–48) and, finally, the French and Indian War, which lasted from 1754 until the Treaty of Paris was signed in 1763 between France and England. During this nearly thirty-year period, the area was the domain of hunters, trappers, explorers, surveyors and rangers/ soldiers, but no permanent settlements were made here by the English due to its remote and exposed location. With the French and English still battling for supremacy in New England and North America, this area was a no-man's-land, remaining vulnerable to attack from the French and their Native American allies. Ironically, the area first gained attention during these wars when soldiers raised from towns in southern and coastal New Hampshire came here. While no actual battles took place in eastern New Hampshire in the territory that is now Carroll County, garrisons were established in the Lake Winnipesaukee area in 1746 by troops who soon became bored. According to historian Georgia Drew Merrill, these troops were idle "and much of the time was spent in fishing and hunting excursions among the mountains…as far north as the Sandwich Range….The soldiers carried back the most glowing reports of the country." Still, the region of Kancamagus and the White Mountains, as historian Russell Lawson states, "remained elusive, unconquered, a vast symbol of timelessness and peace."

Once the peace treaty was signed in 1763, these reports would be remembered by those in southern New Hampshire who were seeking land, and very soon, township grants were being made by New Hampshire's royal governor Benning Wentworth. Of the towns situated along the Kancamagus Highway, the first to be granted were Conway, followed by Albany (originally called Burton until the name was changed in 1833), both in 1766. Slowly but surely, these towns came to be settled, with Conway being the most important. In addition to actually settling the land, one of the first tasks at hand was to build roads. While the first road in Conway was laid out in 1768, it is worth noting that the old Native American trails that had been established many years before in the region also served the first settlers of the White Mountain towns. The first road along the Swift River, the true beginnings of the Kancamagus Highway, came out of Conway Village for but a short distance before entering the town of Albany. This road, however, ran on the north side of the Swift River, not on the southerly side as the highway does today, and connected the Swift River Intervale to the larger and more prosperous town of Conway, where there was a school, a post office and places of business. This road, today known as Dugway or Passaconaway Road, was completed by 1837 and was an important one, though today it is a seasonal road only, maintained by the White Mountain National Forest. It is interesting to note that in 1811 there was a motion at the Conway town meeting to annex part of Albany, but it was voted down. Thus it was that, though Conway would be a prime driver in the development of the Kancamagus Highway, only a mile of its length would run through the town itself.

Albany was described by early historian Georgia Drew Merrill as "a cold, mountainous town with only one tenth its acreage lying in a situation to be tilled." Naturalist Frank Bolles would comment of Albany in 1893 that "Albany knows no priest or physician, squire or shopkeeper, and in its coat of arms, if it had one, the plow and rifle, axe and circular saw, would be quartered with bear and porcupine, owl and grouse....Though their only road to the outside is long and rough, they let no moss gather on it in summer, and no snowdrifts blockade it in winter." It's not surprising that farming in most areas was difficult due to the rocky soil, for the town is home to over a dozen mountain peaks, including the previously mentioned Mount Paugus and Mount Chocorua, as well as South Moat Mountain (2,772 ft.) and Haystack Mountain (2,060 ft.) just north of Dugway Road; the Three Sisters (3,300 ft.), near Champney Falls; and Birch Hill (1,888 ft.), just north of the intervale above Church Ponds. The most populous part of town, South Albany was the gateway to the town and what would later be known as the White Mountain region. However, by 1790, settlers would begin pushing their way west along the Swift River in the northern reaches of Albany and settling the Swift River Intervale, where good farmland was to be found, though the growing season was oh so short. At first, the going was rough. A sawmill was established in 1790, but its proprietor soon abandoned the enterprise. Other settlers also came at this same time, some from Conway, but they, too, would leave after a few short years. The longest to remain here of the early settlers was Austin George, a farmer-teacher who came here from Conway with his wife and fourteen children in 1800, according to historian Charles Beals Jr. They lived in a log home and planted crops of onions, turnips, potatoes and cabbage, the only things that could thrive in the short growing season. Hay was also harvested in abundance for the cattle, but bad weather, a difficulty in getting supplies and the death of several of their children saw the George family leaving the Swift River Intervale in 1815. Life had indeed been hard here, and it would not be until the late 1830s that the area would gain a permanent footing. In 1831, Thomas Russell purchased the land of the abandoned George homestead at auction and built a new home close by the site of the original log cabin. The following year, he sold the land and house to his son, Amzi Russell (1810–77), who would marry Eliza George, a granddaughter of Austin George, in 1834 and move into the house with his new bride. Gradually, a small community of farmers came to be settled in the area known as Passaconaway. Here, a store, school and post office would eventually be established to form a village. In Albany's heyday, during the logging boom of the last decades of the nineteenth century, perhaps 1,500 people lived in Passaconaway at any one time. It's hard to believe that such a population center ever existed along the interior route of the Kancamagus Highway, but it did. Today, the only visible remnants of that settlement still in use, other than the road itself, are the house built by Thomas Russell and his sons, which is a historic site, as well as the Albany Covered Bridge, located about five miles to the east, built by Amzi Russell (to be discussed later on).

Amzi and Eliza Russell would have five children, all girls, during their time together; Martha and Thirza, who grew to be a teacher in the local schools, were the oldest. They were followed by Mary (who died young), Ruth and, lastly, Flora, who was born in 1861 and never married. Russell made a living for his family running a sawmill, located a short distance away on Oliverian Brook. No one knows how this brook got its name for sure, but folklore says that it is a corrupted version of the name Olive

The Albany Covered Bridge as it appeared in the 1960s. *National Archives, courtesy Forest History Society.*

Deering. She is said to have been a young girl who drowned in the brook, probably sometime in the 1830s. Nothing is known of this girl, but she may have been the daughter of James and Nancy Bickford Deering, Nancy being a native of Albany. Russell's sawmill on Oliverian Brook produced over 250,000 feet of board lumber a year, as well as bundles of shingles and clapboards. However, some historians speculate that it may have burned down about 1860. By this time, Russell was heavily invested in buying land in the area, in the hopes that he would make a killing when a railroad was built locally. In 1860, his $5,000 worth of landholdings was five times greater than that of any of his neighbors in Passaconaway, and by 1870 he held some $20,000 worth of land. With surveyors by the late 1830s having laid out a possible rail route from Portland, Maine, to Vermont running right through Albany, he was hopeful of making a huge profit. But his gamble proved a failure. The road from Portland never materialized, and no railroad came to Albany until 1887, ten years after he died. Indeed, by the time of his death, he was so heavily mortgaged that nearly all these lands, nearly nine thousand acres in all, were sold to outside interests to

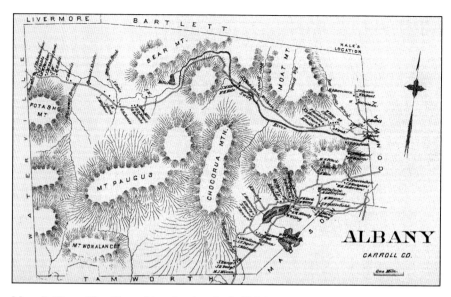

Map of Albany, New Hampshire, showing the Swift River and the Passaconaway settlement at left. *From D.H. Hurd's* New Hampshire State Atlas, 1892.

cover the debt, leaving only the family home and the surrounding land, a little less than three hundred acres in all, to his wife, Eliza.

The home Amzi Russell built with his father would remain in the family for over fifty years after his death. His widow, Eliza, and daughter Ruth Priscilla, who was educated at Wolfeboro Academy (about fifty miles to the south), lived here together for a time until Ruth married Thomas Colbath, a man eight years her junior and the son of a farmer from Wakefield, New Hampshire. When and where they met and how they came to be married, as well as the date of their marriage, is unknown, but perhaps it was when she used to travel to and from school on foot. They were probably married sometime a few years after her father's death, and in 1887 Eliza George Russell deeded the house and land to Ruth and Thomas Colbath, the latter working the land. The valley was so prosperous and populous by 1890, due to both logging and tourism activities, that the Colbath house was made the local post office, with Ruth Colbath serving as postmistress. She would serve in this position until about 1906. Look closely at the front door of the house, and you'll notice a small hinged panel in the center that once served as a mail slot. Ruth Colbath, indeed, was a major figure in the community of Passaconaway and loved her mountain home. However, it does not seem that Thomas Colbath was pleased with rural life, for one day in 1891 he left home, telling his wife, Ruth—according to local lore—that he would

26

be back "in a little while." The time stretched into days, weeks, months and, finally, years, but Colbath remained away, his whereabouts unknown. During this time, Ruth lived with her mother and supported herself by operating a small store, as well as selling off small parcels of the family land for hunting camps. After her mother died in 1905, Ruth even took in boarders during the summer months. During this whole time, Ruth never gave up on her husband and hoped he would return. To that end, she kept a candle burning in the window of her home every night, awaiting his return, and thus the story of her wandering husband became a local legend. Why he left is not known, and not surprisingly, Ruth did not like to talk about the event. She would eventually become known as the "hermit lady" of Passaconaway, as she preferred to remain in her home year-round, and after the tourist season was over, she would eventually become one of the few year-round inhabitants of the area after the logging industry was finished and many local farms were abandoned. From November to May each year, she remained alone, with the exception of one man, Ben Swinston, who lived in a camp a short distance away and helped her with a variety of tasks as needed. Though Ruth Colbath may have been called a hermit, she was really a kind and friendly soul, one who liked talking to seasonal visitors and told of the early settlers who had once lived here. She would also record much of this knowledge, some no doubt gained from her mother, in manuscript form. Ruth Colbath remained a fixture in Passaconaway for decades after her mother died, the last living link to the first settlers of the Swift River Intervale. In early November 1930, she became ill and was taken to Memorial Hospital in North Conway, where she died five days later on November 15. Her body, fittingly, is buried in the original George family cemetery established in the early 1800s and is close to the Kancamagus Highway, easily visible. As for Ruth's husband, Thomas Colbath, she was not wrong. Incredibly, he did indeed return to Passaconaway, but not until 1933, forty-two years after he left and three years after his wife died, the candle in the window long since extinguished. Details about his wandering—some accounts say as far away as the Caribbean—and why he stayed away so long are murky. Why he returned, and what he expected to find in Passaconaway, are also unknown, but what he found was a home that had been sold after his wife's death. Perhaps he returned because it was the time of the Great Depression and he needed a place to stay. Perhaps he wished to make amends to Ruth. Who knows? In any event, he wandered away yet again, and the rest of the details of his life are just as mysterious as the reasons for his having left in the first place. No matter, though, for it is Ruth Priscilla Colbath who deserves to be remembered as one of the most important citizens of Passaconaway, indeed of all those who have lived along the route of the Kancamagus Highway. Every once in a while, I have cause to travel the eastern end of the Kanc through Passaconaway after dark. Several times over the years, I saw an electric candle glowing in the window of the Russell-Colbath House as I passed by and couldn't help but think of Ruth and her life story. It is one of adversity for sure but also one of perseverance and, ultimately, triumph, for she lived life on her own terms in the mountain valley and in the home she so dearly loved.

Of the other individuals who lived in the Swift River Intervale, several are notable for their achievements, and their names are not only enshrined in its lore and legends but are also noted on some of the signs to be seen along the Kancamagus Highway today, or they have geographical features named after them. One such man, all but forgotten today, was covered bridge builder John Douglass. A native of Maine, he arrived here by the late 1840s and was active as a builder, sawmill operator and farmer. He and his wife, Hannah, had five children, including two boys, one of whom drowned in Conway; the other died after his hand was caught in a bear trap. They were neighbors to Amzi Russell and, according to chronicler Charles Beals, Douglass built a dam and a sawmill on a stream that is now named Douglass Brook, which runs in the vicinity of Bear Notch Road. Here he cut timber for his bridge-building activities, which included the old Swift River Bridge in Conway, which lasted from 1850 until raging flood waters destroyed it in the spring of 1869. The current bridge on that same site in Conway was built as a replacement by another builder. Whether Douglass built an earlier covered bridge in Albany is unknown, but he may have offered help and guidance to Amzi Russell when he constructed the present Albany Covered Bridge.

The most important citizen here when it came to the tourist trade was James Shackford, fondly referred to by the patrons of his hotel as Uncle Jim. His father, Thomas, arrived in the intervale early on and was a very successful farmer. James (born 1836), who surely had a vision of the economic future of the White Mountains, turned his family farm into a hotel complex. Indeed, the collection of buildings that were built around his Passaconaway House hotel was the largest group of buildings in the whole area. Shackford and his wife, Hannah, operated the hotel, often just referred to as Shackford's for nearly forty years, and it became a tourist destination in the White Mountains. Not only did he enlarge the family house as the tourist

Fall view of the Swift River northward from the Albany Covered Bridge. *Author photo.*

trade increased, but he also developed the path for tourists, still used today, that leads to nearby Sabbaday Falls. A colorful host, he was said to be "as square as a brick," according to author Charles Beals, and when discussing impending bad weather, was fond of saying about the mountain for which his establishment was named, "When old Passaconaway puts on his nightcap, it's time to run for shelter." At the age of seventy-one, James Shackford, who also served the town in local and state offices, sold his hotel in 1907 and retired. The Passaconaway House operated under new ownership for nine more years until it burned to the ground in February 1916.

Though the White Mountains became a tourist destination after the Civil War, it was still rough and rugged country, a place where hunters, trappers and lumbermen ranged the woods and mountains along today's Kancamagus Highway to make a living. Among those men who were noted for their activities were James "Jack" Allen and Albert "Jigger" Johnson. Allen (1835–1912) was a native of Sebec, Maine, who served as a color-bearer in the Civil War and was severely wounded during the Battle of the Wilderness. After the war, he was a sailor for eight years before coming to the Swift River Intervale in 1873. Though he first worked as an ox driver, according to Charles Beals, he soon made a reputation as a mountain guide and trapper. He boasted that he had been one of the finest shots in the Union army and proved it to those who challenged his skills. He was a man with a larger-than-life personality, known for the supposedly tall tales he told of his hunting adventures, but he was also a kindly man. In addition to his hunting and trapping skills, he also helped cut ice for the Carrigain House hotel, also a fixture in Passaconaway and owned by James Mayhew, a fellow Civil War veteran. Upon Allen's death in 1912, he was buried in the George family cemetery near the Russell-Colbath House, where his simple grave marker may still be seen today.

Renowned hunter, trapper and guide Jack Allen. *From Beals's Passaconaway in the White Mountains, 1916.*

Finally, the Jigger Johnson Campground on the Kancamagus Highway is named after legendary lumberjack and trapper Albert Johnson. Born in 1871, he was a native of Fryeburg, Maine, who made a name for himself working as a lumberman on the Androscoggin River and was legendary as a boss working on the Connecticut River in New Hampshire, according to historian Stewart Holbrook. After his lumbering days were over in the 1920s, the hard-fighting and hard-drinking Johnson became a fire warden for the Forestry Service, manning lookout towers on Mount Chocorua and Carter Dome. However, his drinking got him into trouble, and the Forest Service had to relieve him of his duties. After a couple of other jobs, including a stint with the Civilian Conservation Corps in Maine, he finally settled into a small cabin near Douglas Brook in the Swift River Intervale and lived his final years as a noted fur trapper. This incredibly tough man not only used traps to catch such animals as minks, foxes, fisher cats and bobcats—he also sometimes caught them with his bare hands. In one such adventure, according to author Robert Monahan, Johnson captured two bobcats alive, jumping on them from a tree above while they were feeding on a deer carcass. One of these cats was sold to the University of New Hampshire for fifty dollars to serve as the school's Wildcat mascot. Johnson continued his trapping activities right up until the day he died as a result of an automobile accident while he was on his way to check his traps in the Passaconaway area in March 1935.

Albert "Jigger" Johnson in the White Mountains. *National Archives, courtesy Forest History Society.*

With the loss of such personalities as Jack Allen, Ruth Colbath and Jigger Johnson, coupled with the changing times and end of the lumber trade, the Swift River Intervale gradually lost nearly all of its year-round inhabitants, and the area encompassed by what was later called the Kancamagus Highway became what it is today. It is a scenic mountain area to which tourists flock in great numbers in the summer and fall months, but in the winter and early spring months, it is a snowbound region where wild animals mostly have the mountains all to themselves.

Chapter 3

THE LOGGING RAILROADS
STAKE THEIR CLAIM

A s you drive along the Kancamagus Highway today, there is a seemingly endless expanse of forest, with trees visible as far as the eye can see. To the untrained eye, it might seem as if this forest landscape has always been this way, but if you thought so, you'd be wrong. Once upon a time, from the late 1870s to the 1920s, large expanses of the old-growth forests in the area that would eventually make up the White Mountain National Forest, with many trees 150 years old or more, were cut down during a time when the logging industry reigned supreme. Their time was relatively short, but by the time the lumber barons were done, many areas had been cleared of trees, leaving the landscape barren and rocky. Indeed, what you see today in many areas along the Kancamagus Highway are forests that have recovered since the time commercial logging activities ceased, with trees less than one hundred years old.

When the first settlers came to the area of the White Mountains in the 1760s, one of the most valuable commodities that was readily available was the timber from the forests that surrounded them. Here, trees were there for the taking, used to build homes and barns and provide a source of fuel. However, as had always been the case from early colonial times, the commercial cutting of timber was limited by the means with which this work could be done. Individual farmers or small groups of lumbermen could bring down trees, and numerous sawmills were established in any given locale, but their take was limited to the local economy. To get raw lumber to a larger market, huge teams of oxen and men would have been required, and this was too expensive for the regular landowner. Furthermore, getting those trees out often meant waiting for the wintertime, when sleds could be used. Elsewhere in New Hampshire, large, deep and fast-flowing rivers, like the Connecticut River, could be used for log drives to get huge amounts of timber to market, but in the area of the Kancamagus Highway, this was not possible; the Swift River and other streams were not suitable for large log drives, so it remained a difficult and expensive task to cut timber commercially. Things remained this way until the logging railroads came to the southern White Mountains beginning in the 1870s. As railroad historian Bill Gove has well documented, many of these small railroads were built rather cheaply, and most were never meant to be used more than five years; once an area was logged out, the equipment and tracks were easily removed, sometimes sold or reused elsewhere. The locomotives the logging railroads used were sometimes older and purchased secondhand, though several lines bought new ones. However, according to Gove, while generally operated at a slow speed, they were "capable of surmounting extreme grades of as much as 9 percent and operating on tight curves." The lumber they transported was "carried on two-truck disconnects or on a flat car," and it was by this method that cut timber in large quantities could easily be transported to huge processing lumberyards, such as those located in Conway and Lincoln.

In regard to the lumbermen who cut the trees, dozens of logging camps were established where they had their living quarters in the areas that were being logged. Once an area was logged out, the lumbermen were simply moved to the next area of forest that was being worked by the timber barons. Many of these lumbermen were New Hampshire and Maine men, but many were also French-Canadian immigrants. Some were single men, some brought their families, but either way, life in a lumber camp was a transient affair and could be quite raucous when the men let loose in their off hours. For those who go hiking or bushwhacking in the area of the Kancamagus Highway today, historic remnants of these lumber camps are found quite easily, artifacts ranging from small bottles, cans and other metal items to even an abandoned railroad trestle.

The second-oldest and second-longest-lasting, according to Bill Gove, of the White Mountain logging railroads, and the first established close by the route of the Kancamagus Highway, was the Sawyer River Railroad, which went into operation in 1876 and lasted until 1928. As you travel along the Kanc today, you may notice the town line signs that indicate you have entered the township of Livermore. However, the town in actuality no longer exists and is now considered one of New Hampshire's ghost towns. Two people were counted there in the 2020 federal census, and no one was living there year-round from about the late 1940s to the year 2000. However, back in Livermore's heyday from 1890 to 1900, nearly two hundred people lived there. Livermore was incorporated as a town in 1876, the year the railroad was built, and was solely a company town, its land entirely owned by the Saunders family of Lawrence, Massachusetts. This family was a prominent one in the textile industry centered in that mill town but also sought economic activities further afield. They purchased some thirty thousand acres of timberland in the Pemigewasset Wilderness and in 1874 established the Grafton Lumber Company. It is interesting to note that the Saunders family did practice selective cutting methods, rather than clear-cutting, and thus better preserved the forests in their tracts of land. They established a base of operations in the company town of Livermore (named after a former U.S. senator from New Hampshire and a Saunders relative), which they built and owned. The buildings here included the family mansion (which stood until 1965), as well as a town store, a public hall, a powerhouse and a school. Also located here along the Sawyer River was a sawmill and a railroad engine house and depot, as well as other railroad buildings. The railroad was but eight miles long, its southern terminus being the area just north of Lily Pond near the Kancamagus Highway, several miles east of Kancamagus Pass. The northern terminus was located just northeast of the town of Livermore and met up with the Maine Central Railroad, used to get the company's lumber products to a wider market. The railroad's operations were small, consisting of but one locomotive at any time, which, according to Gove, "had a difficult time staying on the tracks and many accidents resulted." Still, it lasted for many years, finally meeting its end as a result of the historic flood of 1927, a hurricane that hit New England hard in November of that year and devastated many New Hampshire towns. Because the tracks of the Sawyer River Railroad were mostly washed away, operations ceased soon thereafter in 1928. With the railroad gone, the town of Livermore, which is not accessible from the Kancamagus Highway, slowly emptied of people, and the land, now an unincorporated township, soon became a part of the White Mountain National Forest.

The next logging railroad to be established around the Kancamagus was the Bartlett & Albany Railroad, which began operations in 1887. It was owned by the Bartlett Land & Lumber Company, which had been established in the 1870s by a group of men from Portland, Maine. Their line ran from the town of Bartlett, which was a stop on the important Maine Central Railroad, down to the Swift River valley, ending at Passaconaway.

It was a small operation, with only one train used, and was about thirteen miles long; the seasonal Bear Notch Road, the only road that intersects with the Kancamagus Highway, closely parallels the original railroad for part of its length. The railroad ceased operations in 1894, though logging activities would continue until 1904.

Yet another logging railroad to be established in the area, and the largest logging railroad in all of New England, according to Gove, was the East Branch & Lincoln Railroad, based in Lincoln. It was built in 1894 by James Henry and in its heyday would have some seventy-two miles of track. The town of Lincoln (named after an English nobleman, not Abraham Lincoln) was a small and inconsequential place before the railroad and the logging industry came to town. It was granted in 1764 but wasn't settled until 1782. While its population was well under one hundred for most of the nineteenth century, logging operations on a small scale began in the 1850s, and tourists began to come to the area soon after the Civil War. In 1890, just over one hundred people called Lincoln home, but by 1900, with the logging railroad in full-scale operation, that population had soared nearly 400 percent. This railroad was not only the largest of its kind, but it was also the longest lived, continuing in operation under successive owners until the last train ran in 1948. Henry, according to historian Rick Russack, made Lincoln "truly a company town," and he and his sons at one time held all of Lincoln's political offices. While James Henry was an upstanding citizen, and his operations did benefit the town, where a large sawmill and, later, a pulp and paper mill was established, he was also criticized in his day for his clear-cutting operations. While many timber barons of the day followed this same practice of cutting down every tree in a given area, leaving it barren, there were those, like the Saunderses, who selectively cut their lands and did less damage to the environment. Whatever the case may have been, Henry turned the town of Lincoln into an important one. The first logging by Henry's company occurred to the east of Lincoln, heading out of town into the Pemigewasset Wilderness near the route of the Kancamagus. Here, about six logging camps operated from 1892 to 1895. The area immediately west of Kancamagus Pass was clear-cut from about 1894 to 1904, with adjacent areas to the north near Mount Hancock cut as late as 1945. It's hard to realize today, as you begin your drive on the Kanc out of Lincoln, that such a railroad ran through this area and such logging activities ever took place here, though the old locomotive parked in front of the Loon Mountain Resort offers up a large visual hint.

The historic Porter locomotive at Loon Mountain Resort, once used in local logging operations. *Author photo.*

Finally, the eastern end of the Kancamagus Highway would finally see its railroad operations commence in 1906, when the Conway Lumber Company began construction of the Swift River Railroad. This company was a large concern and, despite its local name, was owned and operated by Wall Street industrialist Oakleigh Thorne (1866–1948). Thorne was also a past vice president of Westinghouse and a director of the Wells Fargo Bank, and he held a controlling interest in several New York railroads. As for logging operations in New Hampshire, the company mostly hired contractors, as the owners had little knowledge of the business, according to historian C. Francis Belcher. The company would build a huge sawmill operation complex, with its main building being a modern facility encompassing twenty thousand square feet. This sawmill was located near the modern-day junction of the Kancamagus Highway and New Hampshire Route 16, crossing it and West Main Street and continuing beyond a short distance to the shore of Pequawket Pond. Even before the sawmill was built in 1907, the railroad that would deliver the raw material was constructed by the Boston & Maine Railroad, running from the sawmill site west along the Swift River on its south bank to its headwaters some nineteen miles distant. Overall, the railroad had twenty-six miles of track with several spur lines, including one close to Bear Notch Road and another along Oliverian Brook. This railroad, which delivered its first logs in the summer of 1907, was a large operation, equipped with five locomotives over the years, transporting twenty to twenty-five cars of logs at any given time. As with the other logging railroads in the White Mountains, numerous logging camps were established in the area, with the settlement at Passaconaway becoming the railroad's headquarters. During the ten years the railroad was in operation, Passaconaway and the surrounding area was indeed a beehive of activity, with as many as 1,500 people living there. And then, by 1916, it was all over. With the area logged out, the railroad tracks were pulled up and the rail equipment moved elsewhere on lands being logged by the Conway Lumber Company. As for the sawmill, it remained in operation until its heyday, too, came to an end in 1920. However, locals would take over the site, and smaller operations would continue here for about another forty years. The Swift River Railroad was small and its existence fleeting, but its heritage is an important one, for the Kancamagus Highway runs on its railbed for over half its entire length, right up to its junction with Route 16.

The history of logging and the logging railroads in the White Mountains is an interesting one, with a complicated legacy. It should be noted that almost from the very beginning when these industries were established, there was concern about their impact on the environment and what they would do to New Hampshire's famed mountain scenery. In an 1891 address written by Joseph B. Walker, a member of the state's first forestry commission, he comments,

> *The extension of railroads into the woods, other improved facilities of transportation, and a call for smaller lumber have led, in many instances, to complete denudation in very remote localities....A denuded surface dries quickly, and, if a fire gets well started upon it, its arrest is difficult, if not impossible....After such a burning, a new growth may never start or, if it does, it will be found that portions only of the tract have been reforested.*

While Walker's pleas for better forest management practices went largely unheeded at first, they would eventually pave the way for change with the help of other groups, such as the Appalachian Mountain Club (AMC) and the Society for the Protection of New Hampshire Forests (formed in 1901) and lead to the establishment of the White Mountain National Forest. It is interesting to note that even during the first decades of White Mountain tourism, people were putting old logging roads to use for recreational purposes. The AMC hired individuals like hotelkeeper James Shackford of Passaconaway to cut trails, while even private individuals took the initiative. The current Bolles Trail off the Kancamagus Highway is named for famed nature writer Frank Bolles (1856–94). A native of Massachusetts who worked as a newspaperman and later secretary of Harvard University, he spent much leisure time in Tamworth and hiked the Sandwich Range at all times of the year. In 1891, he opened what he called the "lost trail" with the guidance of local farmer and lumberman Nat Berry on an abandoned logging road that led from Albany to Tamworth. This trail was destroyed in 1915 but was reopened by the Forest Service by 1920 and today serves as the basis for the Bolles Trail. Bolles was well known as a nature writer, and his book *At the North of Bearcamp Water* is a classic in White Mountain literature that is still widely read today. At Bolles's death, an unknown author for the *Harvard Crimson* wrote that Bolles showed "an appreciation of nature, such as perhaps no man has expressed since the time of Thoreau."

That the logging railroads, literally and inadvertently, paved the way for the future development of the Kancamagus Highway is undeniable, and it is fair to ask whether or not this scenic highway might have ever been fully constructed without the earlier development of the Swift River and the East Branch & Lincoln Railroads. While all forestlands in New Hampshire were privately owned by 1867, this situation would change drastically early in the second decade of the twentieth century.

Chapter 4

The Beginnings of the White Mountain National Forest and the Kancamagus Highway

Though extensive logging operations in the White Mountains and the area of the Kancamagus would continue for decades after the turn of the twentieth century, change was coming, and the efforts to save New Hampshire's forestlands would achieve success after years of campaigning by private individuals, local clubs, politicians like former New Hampshire governor Frank Rollins, and nonprofit conservation organizations like the Appalachian Mountain Club, the American Forestry Association and the Society for the Protection of New Hampshire Forests. These efforts came to fruition in a big and meaningful way in February 1911 when the Weeks Act was passed; it was subsequently signed into law by President William H. Taft. This law authorized the purchase of forestland by the government to protect the headwaters of rivers and watersheds in the eastern United States. It has been deemed by many to be one of the most successful conservation acts in our nation's history. The man for whom the legislation was named was Congressman John Wingate Weeks (1860–1926), who was elected to the House from Massachusetts and later was a senator. However, this former naval officer and banker was a New Hampshire man at heart, having been born in Lancaster. He had not only seen firsthand what the logging industry had done to the land, but he also had a summer residence in the mountains of his home state. He first proposed a bill in 1908, which was rejected, but subsequently followed advice from the powerful Speaker of the House, Joseph Cannon of Illinois, to craft a forest preservation bill that a businessman could support. John

W. Weeks got to work and did just that. Though there was much political wrangling, and even opposition from western forest conservation groups that feared their own funding might be reduced, Weeks gained the necessary support for a modified bill, which was passed into law. With the Weeks Act in place, work began very quickly. In March 1911, the White Mountain area was designated a national forest reserve, with boundaries established as to where land could be acquired, and in 1914 the first forestlands were acquired, some seven thousand acres in the town of Benton, southwest of Lincoln. In 1915, more land was acquired, much of it along the future route of the Kancamagus Highway, including the lands west of Livermore to Lincoln and those in the east from Passaconaway to Conway. Indeed, much of the eventual route of the highway was purchased several years before the White Mountains were officially designated a national forest in May 1918. However, the last of the land along the Kanc—running west from Passaconaway, mostly through Livermore but also a small portion through the town of Waterville Valley—would not be acquired until after 1935 due to the logging activities still taking place.

The formal designation of the White Mountain National Forest meant that federal funds were made available, first used for fire-control efforts and eventually for other forestry-related programs and, importantly to our topic, for what were then called forest highways. With a vision in place for preserving and restoring forestlands, fueled by federal funding and other agencies, the reality of a forest highway like the Kancamagus linking Lincoln and Conway was now, more than ever, a possibility. It would take another forty years after the White Mountain National Forest was established to complete the road, the efforts helped in a way by the Great Depression but delayed by World War II.

As might be expected, the railbed of the now-defunct Swift River Railroad would be the first section to be improved. These efforts started in the 1920s. The route was known officially as Forest Highway No. 8 but better known to locals as the Swift River Road, a much more appropriate designation. The going was slow at first, but efforts became more concerted in the 1930s with the establishment of the Civilian Conservation Corps (CCC) camps in the White Mountains. The CCC was established through an executive order by President Franklin D. Roosevelt in April 1933 and was based on a similar program he had established while serving as the governor of New York. These camps were meant to employ some 250,000 men, operating from camps all across the country and working on projects to improve federal lands and government properties. This included such tasks as building trails, roads, bridges and fire lookout towers as well as public campgrounds and other recreation areas. The men of the CCC also worked on flood-control projects, fire prevention and firefighting, as well as many other forestry- and wilderness-related tasks. In return for this work, forty hours a week, they were paid about thirty dollars a month, as well as provided with food, shelter and medical care. Men between the ages of seventeen and twenty-three were eligible, as were certified veterans (who were older and served in separate veteran camps), and signed up for six-month terms of service; they were able to serve a maximum of two years. Each camp employed roughly 200 men, and the camps, organized as companies, were in the charge of reserve army officers. The know-how for the work being performed was provided by camp superintendents, foremen and supervisors who provided guidance for the young men. Never intended as a permanent program but rather as a way to provide meaningful employment during the Great Depression and thus improve morale across the country, it is probably the most famed of Roosevelt's New Deal programs and was one of the most effective until it was finally disbanded in June 1942 due to World War II.

In fact, without the work of the CCC, the eastern end of the Kancamagus Highway would probably have taken longer to develop. During the time of its existence, the CCC established seventeen camps in the White Mountains, including that of the 1177th Company, the Swift River Camp, which was based across the Swift River Road near the Albany Covered Bridge and built

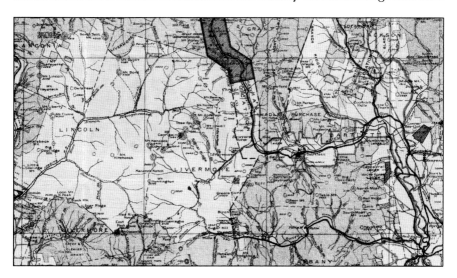

Detail of 1931 map of the White Mountain National Forest. Forest Road No. 8, the future Kancamagus Highway, is shown at bottom. *Library of Congress, G3742.W5 1931 .U5.*

in 1935. This site today is the home of the Blackberry Crossing Campground on the Kancamagus Highway. Just a few miles to the west, a secondary camp was located at Passaconaway. In addition to many forestry and flood-control duties, the men of the CCC helped grade and maintain the Swift River Road and built structures that were used by early tourists on the Kanc and continue to be used today, including the pavilions at Lower Falls and the Passaconaway Campground, as well as a wooden bridge crossing Rocky Gorge. Their work was very important and is celebrated today by historical materials posted at the Saco River Ranger Station and the interpretive signs erected at Blackberry Crossing.

As to the timeline for the building of the Kancamagus Highway, work was begun at both ends in the 1930s but not necessarily with the intent of making it a thruway from Conway to Lincoln. The first contract work on the eventual highway was bid out in 1934, before the CCC was established in the area. The work ran from Conway to Passaconaway, with construction completed to the junction with Bear Notch Road. It should be understood, however, that this work did not include paving the road; rather it consisted of building a solid dirt road that was not by any means intended to carry a heavy traffic load. By 1936, the road upgrades were completed to the Carrol and Grafton County line, just west of the old Shackford homestead and hotel site. At this time, any further work on the eastern end of the Kancamagus ceased until after World War II. This land, running west from Passaconaway and through Livermore, was among the last parcels of land acquired for the White Mountain National Forest in the area along the Kancamagus, and by 1941 it was labeled on maps as the Livermore Wildlife Management Area.

Work on the highway from the Lincoln end got its start in 1937 when surveys were first made. Interestingly, there was originally proposed a different route for the Kancamagus Highway than the one eventually constructed. According to Warren S. Hallamore, the informational representative for the New Hampshire Public Works and Highways Department in 1960, the route first explored on the western end ran southwest from Passaconaway into Waterville Valley and between Tripyramid and Passaconaway Mountains, connecting up with Tripoli Road and running thence to its junction with Daniel Webster Highway (Route 3) several miles south of North Woodstock. This route would have been an interesting one, but it bypassed the town of Lincoln altogether and surely was opposed by the business interests there. Tripoli Road remains to this day well worthy of travel, but it is still a scasonal road that is closed in the winter.

U.S Forest Service steam shovel at work on the Kancamagus Highway in the 1930s. *National Archives, courtesy Forest History Society.*

In any event, construction from the west was contracted out and begun in 1938, running about seven and a half miles westward. While this part of the Kancamagus was not built on any former railroad bed, the activities of the East Branch & Lincoln Railroad for many years previously made access to the wilderness possible. This section of the highway, terminating at the North Fork of the Hancock Branch stream (just west of the hairpin turn) was completed in 1939 at a cost of just over $196,000, several thousand dollars under budget. Further construction was planned in 1940–41, but with the coming of World War II, all physical work on the highway was stopped. This is not surprising, as the men required for the work, as well as equipment, fuel and other supplies (including oil and tires), were all limited by wartime restrictions. However, discussions in New Hampshire political circles would continue about the highway and its possibilities. Though it was still rated as a secondary road, research by Keith Osborne shows that in 1943 the first discussions about the highway regarding the possibility of linking Conway and Lincoln, primarily as a "timber access route," were being had between forestry officials and state legislative representative Sherman Adams, a Republican from Lincoln who would become the Speaker of the House by 1944. Tourism, it would seem, was not on the minds of the decision-makers just yet, but that would eventually change, and Sherman Adams would be a major force behind the future development of the Kancamagus Highway.

Chapter 5

THE COMPLETION OF THE KANCAMAGUS HIGHWAY AND THE INFLUENCE OF LOON MOUNTAIN

A fter the end of World War II in August 1945, construction would eventually resume on the Kancamagus Highway, though it was not yet known by that name. Just when the construction resumed is not certain, but there was likely a delay of several years, perhaps as many as three or four. This is quite understandable; while many men would return home after hostilities ended, many were left overseas, both in Europe and in Japan, as part of the occupation forces. No matter what the reasons, it would take over a decade for the highway to be completed, even if the number of miles remaining to be constructed was relatively small. By 1951, the small section from Passaconaway to the Waterville Valley town line was completed, while construction at the Lincoln end from the area of the North Fork had also started. Now the most difficult section of the highway's construction was beginning, and four years later real progress had been made. From the Lincoln end, construction of the hairpin turn and just beyond, ascending Kancamagus Pass, was underway. Meanwhile, construction crews from the east had made their way into Livermore, progressing just past Lily Pond, and by 1956 just a one-mile gap remained to complete the highway linking Conway and Lincoln.

Why did it take so long to construct these few remaining miles of the highway? Well, as the research of Keith Osborne demonstrates, this last section of the highway was extremely difficult to build. The two main contractors on the project are said to have gone into bankruptcy, likely because the amount they had bid to win the contract was too low. Remember,

The C.L. Graham Wangan Overlook, 1961. Note how narrow the early highway was. *National Archives, courtesy Forest History Society.*

this was no small project, even if the road was initially an unpaved secondary one, and so the logistics were especially challenging. Men, materials and heavy equipment had to be transported into a remote region, and the amount of rock that had to be removed to cut the road through the mountains was huge, as was the amount of fill needed to build the roadbed. It was also true that funding for the project, or lack thereof, sometimes determined the pace of the work. Between construction challenges and delays of all types, the final mile progressed slowly.

Meanwhile, it was in 1957 that the road was officially named the Kancamagus Highway and it became part of the state's secondary highway system, with maintenance assumed by the state. As to the choice of the name, this was not accomplished without some debate and controversy in the New Hampshire State House. Some questioned whether it was appropriate to name the highway after a man who led the raid on the settlement at Dover that resulted in the brutal death of Major Richard Waldron, an important figure in the state's colonial history. However, Representative Robert Monaghan from the town of Hanover argued in favor of Kancamagus the man and also commented, "I'll admit that the name may be a bit difficult, but it's easier to spell than Winnipesaukee and easier to pronounce than Chocorua." In the end, the name was an appropriate one, not only honoring the last leader of the Native Americans who had called the area home long before Europeans arrived but also keeping in character with the naming practices of the peaks in the southern White Mountains, as well as other geographical features in Carroll County. Just as our Founding Fathers were given their due respect in the naming of the peaks of the Presidential Range to the north, the naming of the Kancamagus Highway gave historic Native American leaders that same respect.

In 1958, work on the last remaining mile began, and finally, in the summer of 1959, the highway was completed. With no formal announcement or any organized celebration, the highway was open to through traffic. Interestingly, at this same time, the first section of the highway out of Conway was upgraded, and by the end of 1960, the first eleven miles had been paved with asphalt and the road and its narrow shoulders and bridges widened. However, the rest of the unpaved road had its limitations and was still not the highway we know today. The Kancamagus was at first only open to traffic during the daytime hours and was closed at night. It was also, like a number of wilderness roads in New Hampshire—such as the previously mentioned Tripoli Road, as well as the Sandwich Notch Road farther to the south—strictly a seasonal road and closed in the wintertime. During this time, it seems that access to the road was blocked in the late fall season simply by placing large boulders across the entrance of the road at either end. One local resident would, years later, recount to Joseph Phillips, visitor information supervisor at the Saco River Ranger Station, that he was able at times to squeeze his Volkswagen Beetle between these rocks and was thereby able to travel the highway, at least until the winter snows came.

Despite these limitations, and though the highway was not heavily publicized by the state at first, news spread rapidly, and soon enough, volume on the Kancamagus Highway increased. This is not surprising, for several reasons. First and foremost, the views of the White Mountains from the highway were now not only spectacular but also easily accessible to all. It used to be that to gain such views, a person would have to be an experienced hiker to make a difficult trek into the wilderness, but no longer. On a wider scope, the 1950s was also a booming time in America. The postwar economy was in overdrive, and Americans were buying consumer goods at a record pace as a result of the pent-up demand due to wartime rationing and restrictions. The auto industry was a big beneficiary, with

Early view, circa 1961, of the hairpin turn, with the Hancock Overlook and Osceola Range in the background. *National Archives, courtesy Forest History Society.*

sales quadrupling in the ten-year period beginning in 1945. Indeed, by the time the Kancamagus Highway was completed as a through road, nearly 75 percent of all households in America owned at least one car. Despite initial fears, jobs were also plentiful after the war ended, and with the added benefits of the GI Bill, many men trained for new careers. And those careers came, in many instances, with vacation time. And so it was, with all these combined factors, that Americans hit the road and traveled to places near and far like they never had before to see all the sites our country had to offer. It was the golden age of American travel, when roadside motels and attractions popped up everywhere, and the modern American station wagon was the family vehicle of choice until it was replaced by the minivan in the 1980s. Yes, the Kancamagus Highway was completed at just the right time, but more work was yet to be done. In fact, less than a year after the Kancamagus Highway was completed, Warren Hallamore of the New Hampshire Public Works and Highway Department offered up a warning. Even though over $2 million had been spent to build the road since 1934,

Early damage on the Kancamagus Highway. *National Archives, courtesy Forest History Society.*

he stated that "presently, it is a steep-graded, narrow-shouldered, often tightly winding gravel road and because funds are not available to maintain it properly as a 'good road,' excessive traffic could soon make it hazardous." It is interesting to note that the state and the White Mountain National Forest even minimized signage at either end to keep the number of travelers low on the new highway, though it is clear that word of mouth soon enough spread the word about its scenic beauty. Highway officials also worried that "any breakdown or serious accident could be disastrous due to a lack of communication," as the Kancamagus was uninhabited for most of its length.

For most of its history, the road that eventually became the Kancamagus Highway was a tale of two towns, Albany and Conway in the east. However, the final focus on the evolution of the highway came from the west and the town of Lincoln. While the town had been the center of large and profitable timber and paper mill operations since the late 1800s, times had changed, and those industries were in decline. Between 1940 and 1950, the town saw a decrease in its population of 9.3 percent as industry faded, and in the succeeding decade, during which the Kancamagus Highway was completed as a through road, that population decreased yet again by just over 13 percent. While the town was in economic decline and its fortunes looked bleak, there was one man who had a vision and refused to let Lincoln's prosperity fade away. His name was Sherman Adams (1899–1986), and though he was not a native of New Hampshire, he is a legendary figure not only in the history of Lincoln but also in New Hampshire and national politics. His story is one of hard work, power and influence in politics at the highest level but also of his love for skiing, his adopted hometown and the mountains that surround it.

Llewelyn Sherman Adams was born in East Dover, Vermont, and graduated from high school in Providence, Rhode Island. He subsequently attended Dartmouth College in Hanover, New Hampshire, where he was very active with the Dartmouth Outing Club, according to writer Greg Kwasnik, setting records in his hiking activities. Adams graduated in 1920 after having served in the Marine Corps during World War I and that summer worked with the Appalachian Mountain Club on a trail-building crew. A short while later, he found employment in Vermont, where he married his wife, Rachel White, in Rutland in the summer of 1923. The couple soon thereafter moved to New Hampshire, where their first child was born in 1924. The Adamses settled in Lincoln, where Sherman was employed as timberlands manager by the Parker-Young Company, which had purchased the East Branch & Lincoln Railroad in 1917. Sherman Adams, with his great love of the outdoors, first served the company, managing their many logging camps as a "walking boss." He was a short, wiry, rugged young man who, though still learning the trade, was willing to jump right in and perform any task. His character was that of a typical Yankee: blunt, with a dry sense of humor and not always easy to get along with. He even described himself to his mother as one who was "an external crab without grace, manners, or considerations." Still, he usually gained the respect of all who worked with him and came to know him. Adams worked in the logging business for nearly twenty years, but with the realization, perhaps, that the business was one that was slowly fading away, he turned to another pursuit—politics. He first ran for and won a seat in the New Hampshire State House as a Republican in 1941, and after three years he became the Speaker of the House. His political star on the rise, Adams subsequently won a seat in the U.S. House, representing New Hampshire from 1945 to 1947, then made his first run for governor but lost. He ran again and won, serving two terms as governor from 1949 to 1953 (New Hampshire terms lasting two years, unlike most states). During his time in office, he managed the state well and kept its budget balanced during difficult times. However, his organizational talents also garnered him recognition on the national stage; he managed Dwight D. Eisenhower's New Hampshire presidential campaign in 1952, as well as campaigning for him nationwide and being the floor manager at the Republican National Convention. Indeed, Adams was just as adept at managing delegates from all over the country as he was at dealing with rough-and-tumble lumberjacks in his earlier years. It was for this reason that Dwight Eisenhower chose him for his chief of staff as he began his presidency in 1953.

During his time in the Eisenhower administration, Sherman Adams developed the role of the modern presidential chief of staff, and by doing so he became one of the most powerful men in the country—and probably the most powerful chief of staff in history. He controlled access to the president and thus helped control the domestic agenda. He was quick to say no to those who came to him with ideas for the president, thus gaining the nickname "the Abominable No Man." A liberal Republican, Adams was the subject of much ire from both sides of the political aisle. Democrats, of course, opposed Eisenhower, and Adams was their public villain as he spoke on behalf of the president, keeping Eisenhower above the fray. Conservative Republicans, too, had their problems with the administration, with the president and Adams deciding that the activities of Senator Joseph McCarthy, he of the Army-McCarthy hearings and communist witch hunts, must be blunted.

Adams was a key figure in President Eisenhower's first term and helped him get elected to a second. However, less than two years into Eisenhower's second term, Adams got embroiled in a scandal that cost him his job. He was forced to leave his position in October 1958 when it became public knowledge that he had accepted the gift of an expensive coat from a wealthy Boston manufacturer who was then under investigation by the Federal Trade Commission. The look, of course, was not a good one, so Sherman Adams was fired and returned home to New Hampshire. Ultimately, nothing else came of the incident, and Eisenhower's loss would soon prove to be New Hampshire's gain.

Sherman Adams returned to his home in Lincoln and settled into retirement, taking up the hiking and skiing activities he had always loved. He also came home to a town that was in decline and realized that tourism would have to be the answer. The question was: What would bring tourists to town? Unlike elsewhere in the White Mountains, there was no skiing industry here to bring in hordes of visitors. Luckily, Adams's wife, Rachel, pushed him

A station wagon making its way through the birches on the Kancamagus Highway, circa 1961. *National Archives, courtesy Forest History Society.*

Early postcard view of the Kancamagus Highway in winter, circa 1960. *Author collection.*

to action, telling him, "There must be a place to ski up there somewhere. What are you going to do about it?" Well, Adams went back to his old days of roving the mountains, doing so in the wintertime in snowshoes. One day a few years after returning home, after having climbed Loon Mountain, he had his answer, for here was a peak with the perfect attributes for a ski resort. And so, Sherman Adams found a new project and tackled it head-on, even if it was not accepted by everyone in town at first. Though Adams had returned to New Hampshire in disgrace, he still had a lot of connections and could draw on some political clout. Not only did Adams gain permission for Loon Mountain from the U.S. Forest Service after two years of negotiations, he also persuaded the Army Corps of Engineers to cancel a project in the area. In addition, he worked tirelessly to gain investors and funding for his Loon Mountain Recreation Company.

Importantly to our subject, Sherman Adams also realized that tourists needed a way to get to his new mountain resort. To that end, he lobbied hard to get Lincoln an exit off the new I-93 interstate highway that was being built, something which, as Greg Kwasnik wrote, "would soon make Loon one of the most accessible resorts in New England." Adams also worked with the New Hampshire Public Works to get the Kancamagus Highway recognized as a state highway, complete with its own route number; it was officially designated as Route 112. Around this same time, in 1964, the Kancamagus Highway was also fully paved to prevent any further deterioration, though it still remained a seasonal road and was closed at night. Sherman Adams

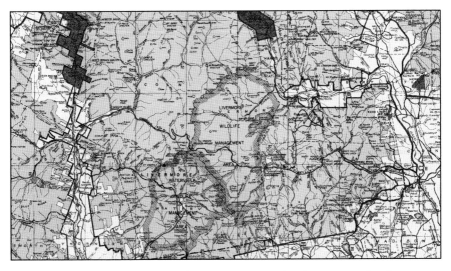

A 1963 map of the White Mountain National Forest showing the now-completed Kancamagus Highway (*center*). *Library of Congress, G3742.W5E63 1963 .U5.*

Early view of the Kancamagus Highway and the Osceola Range, circa 1960. *National Archives, courtesy Forest History Society.*

opened the Loon Mountain resort to skiers in December 1966 and viewed the Kancamagus Highway as a way to bring in skiers from the east who could enjoy what North Conway's mountains had to offer on one day and Loon Mountain, thirty-five miles to the west, on another day during the same trip. Others in New Hampshire's state government now had the same vision, and so it's no coincidence that in 1968, a year after Loon Mountain opened, the Kancamagus Highway was opened to twenty-four-hour traffic and would be maintained all year-round.

What had started as a simple country road running from Conway and Albany in the east in the 1790s eventually, after 178 years, had become one of the premier scenic byways in New England, and now millions of people travel the road annually to enjoy the mountain wilderness of New Hampshire. While many today may lament the march of so-called progress in many human building endeavors through our history, such is not the case with the Kanc, for forestry and conservation advocates and tourists alike can all agree that the Kancamagus Highway is a thing of beauty.

PART II

A Guide to Driving the Kancamagus Highway

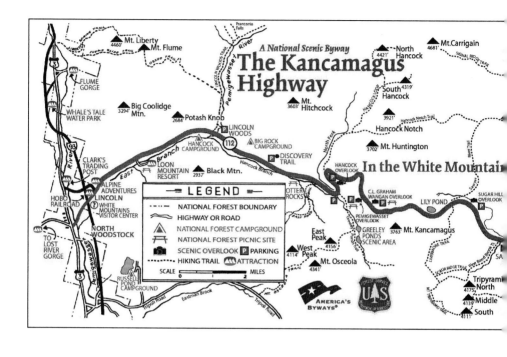

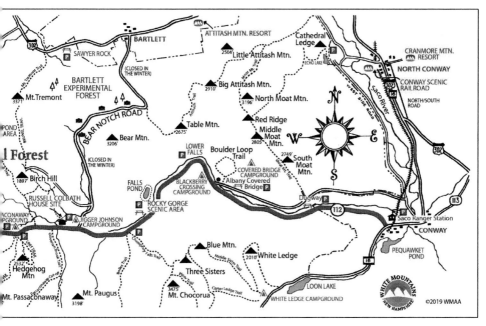

Modern map of the Kancamagus Highway showing all the scenic and historic attractions. *Courtesy White Mountain Attractions Association.*

Chapter 6

SCENIC ATTRACTIONS
ALONG THE KANC

I n this section, we will take a look at the scenic and historical sites located directly along the Kancamagus Highway, starting at Conway in the east and running westward to Lincoln and North Woodstock. Campgrounds, with the exception of the one at Blackberry Crossing, and extended hiking trails that are found along the highway will be covered in separate chapters. The sites in this chapter are all easily accessible to most visitors—though there are some limitations to people who have disabilities—at most times of the year. In the wintertime and early spring, however, some of these areas are closed, so if you're coming to the highway during this time, please check in advance. Visitors can check out the White Mountain National Forest website at https://www.fs.usda.gov/whitemountain for the most up-to-date information. Perhaps the most frequently asked question about the highway is: How long will it take me to travel the Kancamagus? There is no single answer to that question. If you are traveling its entire length, without stopping and getting out of the car, it will generally take you less than an hour, depending on the traffic and the weather. However, if you plan on stopping at some of the overlooks (and why wouldn't you?!) with the goal of taking some pictures, your time could stretch out considerably longer, perhaps adding another hour or two to your journey. Of course, if you plan on stopping at every site, or plan on doing some hiking from trailheads off the Kanc, you may need the entire day, and then some, to accomplish your goals. In the end, it's all about what you want to experience. To that end, the

"No gas" notice with Potash Knob (2,684 ft.) in the background on the west end of the Kancamagus Highway. *Author photo.*

section at the end of this book offering tips and information to those planning on driving the Kancamagus Highway will be helpful and provide additional guidance to visitors who are not familiar with the road or the White Mountain National Forest, its policies and what it has to offer. Finally, please note that while all listed information is current as of this writing, it is subject to change.

Saco River Ranger Station

What to Know

This station, the most visited ranger station in the White Mountain National Forest, is located at 33 Kancamagus Highway in Conway. Upon entering the Kanc from Route 16, it is almost immediately on the right. This station is a perfect place to start your journey and is the only ranger station on the Kanc open year-round, every day. Inside, there are friendly and knowledgeable rangers who can answer your questions and offer guidance. It is open on Mondays from 9:00 a.m. to 4:30 p.m. and Tuesday through Sunday from 8:00 a.m. to 4:30 p.m. Not only are maps and other historical materials available here for viewing, but there is also a section of local books, guides and maps available for purchase. Most importantly, you can also buy here the passes required to enter certain recreational areas along the highway. These passes can also be purchased in advance online at https://www.myscenicdrives. com/store/#nh-white-mountain. If you don't purchase in advance, I highly recommend buying your pass here if you plan on visiting all the sites along the highway. The cost is thirty dollars, and a pass is good for one year from the date of purchase. Your other option is to self-purchase a day pass at each site you visit. These cost five dollars; you place the money in an envelope available at a paybox at each site and the stub on your windshield. All of this is done on the honor system, but rangers regularly patrol these sites, and if you have no pass or have not made a payment, a citation will be issued, the current fine being eighty-five dollars. If you don't plan on visiting every site, this cumbersome option may be the one for you, but otherwise it's just easier to buy the pass, stick it on your windshield, and then you have nothing more to worry about. I should also note that several historic sites along the Kanc do have signs showing a QR code that can theoretically be scanned to buy a pass. Unfortunately, these signs are a bit misleading, as there is no cell phone service that enables such a transaction! For other traveling logistics, the ranger station also has nice public restrooms, though they are not fully accessible to people with disabilities.

Points of Interest

While you may be anxious to begin your trip, during good weather, take the time to check out the viewing garden in front and to the side of the station.

It was first planted in 2008 and features nearly one hundred species of plants that are native to the White Mountain region and found in its woodland, meadow or transitional sites. There are also three interpretive pictorial sign panels that educate and inform the nature lover about the plants' names, habitats and pollinators. One interesting aspect of this garden is the fact that the seeds from the plants grown here are collected, dried and stored, ready to be used on reclamation projects in the White Mountain National Forest.

Upon turning right after leaving the Saco River Ranger Station, your next destination, the Albany Town Forest, is just .6 miles down the road on the right, just before the Conway-Albany town line.

Albany Town Forest Hiking Trails

What to Know

This site, whose simple sign is small and easy to miss, is located .7 miles from the junction of the Kancamagus Highway and Route 16, on the right. It consists of 5.2 miles of interconnecting walking-hiking-biking trails, all of which are wide, flat, with little elevation and rated as being easy to hike.

Points of Interest

There are four trails here; the 1.5-mile Davis Farm Trail runs the entire length of the town forest, winding through the woods as well as the Swift River floodplain. The Swift River Trail is perhaps the most scenic and well worth a stop alone, being 1.5 miles long and offering a close-up view of the banks of the Swift River, with which you will become even more acquainted as you journey on the Kanc. It combines with the Davis Farm Trail to form a 3-mile loop. The Trestle Trail is also very interesting; it passes through open and active farmland close to the junction of the Swift and Saco Rivers and offers a view of the old iron railroad bridge, a Baltimore-truss structure built from 1906 to 1907 and used today by the Conway Scenic Railroad. The other trail here is the Uphill-Both-Ways Trail, a 1-mile biking loop.

Historical Information

This is a new trail system established in 2012 on lands owned by the Town of Albany in cooperation with the Upper Saco Valley Land Trust and the Trust for Public Land. It was chosen as the winner by *New Hampshire Magazine* in its annual Best of New Hampshire rankings in 2014 in the multiuse trail category. The concept of a "town forest" has its origins in early colonial New England, when all towns had forests and public lands that were available for use by all settlers. Early on, timber was also harvested from town forests to build public buildings, as well as to sell to cover town expenses. Today, many towns in New Hampshire, including Albany, continue to have town forests, many of which now serve as recreational spaces. Though not affiliated with the Albany Town Forest, the White Mountain National Forest operates on these same principles—that its lands are the people's lands—only on a larger scale.

As you turn right out of the Albany Town Forest and head west on the Kanc, you will pass the last vestiges of any built-up town area before entering the wilderness from Conway into Albany. Your next stopping point is 5.5 miles ahead. Remember that you're traveling on the former roadbed of the Swift River Railroad, so it is straight and easy going, mostly through the woods at first. Though the Swift River is just a short distance away on your right, it is not visible right off. This was by design, so that the railroad (and later the Kancamagus Highway) would not be endangered by possible flooding of the Swift River in an area close to its junction with the Saco River just a few miles distant. Early Native Americans knew it was wise not to build their villages so close to river floodplains, though later settlers often learned the hard way when it came to their homesites. These first 2.5 miles of the Kanc before you enter the White Mountain National Forest may seem a bit uninteresting, and they have historically been so, even when the main road was located on the opposite side of the Swift River. The 1880 White Mountain guidebook and "handbook for travelers" edited by Moses Sweetser and published in Boston stated that "the road is very dull until it passes Allen's Mill, since it runs through deep forests. There is no public conveyance." This last statement referred to the fact that there was no public stagecoach at that time and that travelers were on their own or had to rely on carriage service provided by hotels, like Shackford's Passaconaway House, where they were staying. Getting back to modern-day travel, it's not long before you pass the sign that denotes the highway's status as a National Scenic Byway. The

Entering the White Mountain National Forest from the western end of the Kancamagus Highway on a fall day. *Author photo.*

highway gained this status in 1996; the designation means that the road does not just take drivers from here to there but is a destination drive in and of itself, which will soon become apparent. Soon enough, the Swift River again makes its appearance, and from here on out there are several pull-off areas where you can park and get out of your vehicle and walk a short distance to get a better view of the river.

Albany Covered Bridge

What to Know

As you turn into this site, which requires a pass to visit, you have two options; you may park in the front parking lot and visit the bridge on foot. Or, if your vehicle is less than seven feet, nine inches in height, you can drive across the bridge and park in a lot on Dugway/Passaconaway Road

Left: Fall view of the Albany Covered Bridge from the Swift River downstream. *Author photo.*

Below: View of the eastern portal of the Albany Covered Bridge. *Author photo.*

located just a short distance from the bridge to the right. Most passenger cars, trucks and SUVs can make the crossing, but beware: if you're driving a commercial or recreational vehicle with a greater height or a weight in excess of the posted tonnage, you will not be able to use the bridge. If in doubt, do not attempt to enter the bridge. Ideally, for the fullest experience, take the time to travel the bridge both by vehicle and on foot. When on foot, you will have the time and opportunity to enjoy and photograph both the upriver and downriver views from inside the bridge, even when the tourist season is in full swing and the place is packed with visitors, as well as check out its unique interior construction. As you make your drive, be on guard; while there are several traffic signs around the bridge, please be sure to be polite to other drivers and take your turn entering the bridge slowly, doing so with your lights on so oncoming traffic from the opposite end can see you. In addition, please be mindful of pedestrians that may be walking all around you within the bridge. The banks of the river on both sides are fairly easily accessible from both parking areas, and one can even wade into the river to get a good view of the bridge, though care should be exercised when climbing across the slippery rocks.

Points of Interest

Traveling over the bridge by vehicle is a unique sensation, one that many people don't get to experience all that often these days. Think about it for a minute: Can you imagine the time long ago when a horse and rider, a stagecoach or a horse-drawn wagon were the main users of this bridge? The main sounds to be heard in this bygone era, other than the water gurgling over the rocks below, were the clip-clop of horseshoes and the creaking of wagon wheels. It's not hard to conjure up such an image while going through the bridge at a slow pace. Of course, at night, such a crossing in the old days was an entirely different experience, as the bridge had no lights to guide travelers. As you take a walk through the interior of the bridge, the second-oldest man-made structure to be found along the Kancamagus Highway, note the off-kilter boxed X panels that make up its truss support system, as well the laminated arches on each side, which offer additional support. Other things to look for in the bridge, if you're so inclined, are the thousands of tree nails or trunnels, the wooden pegs used to hold the bridge together long before metal bolts were used, as well as the huge laminated arches, which are many layers thick. Even if you're

View of the Swift River downstream from the interior of the Albany Covered Bridge. *Author photo.*

The Albany Covered Bridge portal, at the end of Dugway/Passaconaway Road, circa 1961. *National Archives, courtesy Forest History Society.*

not a woodworker, it's easy to appreciate the bridge technology of the 1850s. Many visitors today may view this covered bridge as a quaint relic of days gone by, but when it was built, the covered bridge was a tried-and-true form in New England and beyond. Interpretive signs that have been erected close to the bridge on either side provide further interesting details about its construction, as well as some of the history of the area, that are helpful to visitors who want to know more. The greatest joy for many will be the stunning views of the Swift River, both from within the bridge as well as from along its banks with the bridge as a main focal point—a true photographer's paradise.

Historical Information

This site on the Kancamagus is noted for its bridge architecture, natural beauty and historical importance. It is at this point that the first road into the Swift River Intervale, Dugway Road (also known as Passaconaway Road) from Conway, crossed the Swift River. The road was completed in 1837 and led to the economic development of the area. It was natural that it would cross here due to the geography of the river itself, which loops northward from just beyond this point, skirting the base of Bear and Moat Mountains. It made more sense to cross the river here in relatively straight-line fashion, rather than follow the river's north bank to cut a longer road making the same distance. We don't know much about the first bridge built at this site; at first it was likely a simple plank bridge, but as the Passaconaway settlement grew, another, sturdier, bridge was sorely needed. In any case, the first bridge on this site was built by Amzi Russell in 1857; it was destroyed by a windstorm in 1858. Russell rebuilt the bridge that same year with help from Leandre Morton. The two were paid $1,300 by the Town of Albany for the project, less the cost of the original bridge, which is unknown. How much money Russell actually made on the two-bridge project is unknown, but it was unlikely a large sum. In any case, his second bridge was well constructed, has had better luck and has remained standing now for 164 years. In 1970, the bridge received a substantial rehabilitation, and from 1981 to 1982 its wooden floor timbers were replaced with steel by the U.S. Forest Service. Despite the bridge's remote location, the Kancamagus Highway brings thousands of tourists to visit every year.

View of rock ledges above the Kancamagus Highway from the Lower Falls Scenic Area. *Author photo.*

This bridge is interesting to the covered bridge enthusiast for its design. There were many truss designs used in covered bridges all over the United States, but this one employs a truss variant that was designed right here in New Hampshire by a man named Peter Paddleford of Littleton. Though never patented, the truss became a popular one among builders in New Hampshire's North Country and was used extensively in the Conway area, as well as in the nearby towns of Jackson, Bartlett, Ossipee and Sandwich, as well as in Fryeburg and Porter, Maine, and here in Albany, with nine examples in all still standing in these towns. In fact, most bridges of this type are found in northern New Hampshire, with the exception of a few others in eastern Vermont and one far-flung example in Ohio, so they're a bit of a rarity in comparison with other types of covered bridges.

Turn right out of the parking lot for the Albany Covered Bridge, and almost directly across the highway is your next destination on the Kanc.

Blackberry Crossing Campground

What to Know

Located just across the highway from the Albany Covered Bridge, this campground is included here because it contains an interesting and important historic site. This site within the campground is easy to find; it is adjacent to the parking lot located to the left after turning onto the campsite road from the Kancamagus and has interpretive panels that tell the story of the CCC. Details regarding the campsites here are provided in chapter 8.

Historical Information

This campground was established on the grounds of the former Civilian Conservation Corps camp that was built here in 1935. Perhaps several thousand young men in all called this place home for a time during its years of existence. They performed all manner of forestry, maintenance and construction work along the highway in the White Mountain National Forest during their terms of service until the CCC was disbanded in mid-1942. In fact, nine buildings were constructed for the camp, including four barracks, built Army-style, which housed fifty men each. The other buildings included a headquarters building, a mess hall/kitchen to feed the men daily, an infirmary for those needing medical care and a recreational hall that also served as a study hall. There was also an outdoor boxing ring, as well as a motor-pool facility for the camp's utility vehicles. Though all of the buildings are now long gone, one lone stone chimney remains standing, a silent sentinel to attest to the men who stayed here and served their country.

After making a left turn out of Blackberry Crossing to continue westward, you have but .6 miles to go before you reach the most visited spot on the Kancamagus Highway.

LOWER FALLS SCENIC AREA

What to Know

This site is the most visited on the Kancamagus and in all of the White Mountain National Forest—and for good reason. Here, at a bend in the Swift River, is a beautiful waterfall that is easily accessible and viewable for all. The site, which requires a pass, has ample parking, some eighty spaces, and roadside parking is also available in designated spots. Lower Falls is popular not just for its beautiful scenery but also because it is a popular swimming destination in the summertime. In fact, among all the natural swimming spots in the White Mountains and throughout New Hampshire, this is probably one of the most visited. If you are coming here to swim in the summer, plan on arriving early, as parking spots will quickly be occupied. With public restrooms and picnic tables and charcoal grills on the site, it is a fun place to spend the day swimming and picnicking. Throughout much of July and August, a Forest Service worker is stationed here to offer guidance and sell passes, as well as act as a contact for those who suffer injuries, but please know that there are no lifeguards, and swimmers should be careful and know their own limitations. Lower Falls is typically less crowded during peak periods on weekdays and in slower times in the spring and late fall before and just after Columbus Day weekend. It should be noted that the Lower Falls parking lot and its facilities are closed from late fall until mid-May, but one can park in an area just in front of the gate and still access the site if weather permits, though the area and its path will not have been maintained.

Points of Interest

The falls here are gradual; the water drops many feet until it reaches a broad pool, which has been carved out over millions of years of glaciation and water flow action. The water runs throughout much of the year, even during the dry season, and one can wade easily into the water to stand among the rocks or swim in the natural pool during the summertime. It is quite the experience, though care must be exercised so as not to slip on the rocks and during times when the water runs high. In the off-season when it's too cold to swim, one can usually venture out onto the rocks to get a close-up view of the falls without getting too wet. There is a trail along the water that gives close-up views of the falls from several vantage points, so stopping here is a must-see experience. Take note of the wood pavilion as well; it was built by the CCC in the 1930s, one of their many contributions to the tourist experience along the Kancamagus. While the falls are beautiful to photograph, if you'd like to get a shot of them without people, your task will be a difficult one during the peak summer and fall months, especially on the weekends.

Historical Information

Unlike other sites, like Rocky Gorge and Sabbaday Falls, Lower Falls was not well known during the early years of White Mountain tourism activity. This was because the original Swift River Road built here was located somewhat farther away from the river. However, this changed in the 1930s when the course of the road was altered to follow the old railbed of the Swift River Railroad. From that time forward, Lower Falls quickly grew in popularity, and the rest, as they say, is history.

As you turn right out of the parking lot here and continue westward toward Lincoln, the distance to Rocky Gorge is a short one, 2.2 miles, but the views of the Swift River are excellent.

ROCKY GORGE SCENIC AREA

What to Know

The Rocky Gorge Scenic Area is another must-see water site along the Kancamagus Highway. The parking lot is large, though crowded at peak times, and a pass is required. Public restrooms are available. There is a wooded trail along the Swift River that leads to a path that takes you to Rocky Gorge (sometimes also called Upper Falls); the going is pretty easy, and there are many excellent views of the river along the way. As you approach the gorge on the designated pathway, depending on the time of year and the water levels, there are ample opportunities for those who are sure of foot to diverge from the path and walk out onto the rocks. Note that while swimming is allowed upriver, it is not permitted in the gorge itself. Given all there is to see and experience at the Rocky Gorge Scenic Area, a stop here could last well over an hour if you choose to make the Falls Pond hike.

Points of Interest

Here you can view the narrow, deeply cut channel that leads to the gorge itself. At certain times of the year, you will notice driftwood and other debris along the riverbank, giving a clear indicator of how high the aptly named Swift River can rise—and for good reason. The gorge is a ten-foot drop into a pool below in which, even at the driest times of the year, the water is roiling. To get a good look at the channel both upstream and downstream, go on the footbridge that crosses Rocky Gorge. The scenic views upriver are spectacular, as is the gorge itself, carved out by thousands of years of water action over and around the granite riverbed. Visit Rocky Gorge in the fall and it may seem fairly tame, but check it out after a heavy rainfall or in the spring when the snow melt-off is still occurring, and you'll be surprised at the difference. Be sure to spend plenty of time checking out the river and the gorge itself, but afterward, there is even more to see. After crossing the Rocky Gorge footbridge, it is but a short walk to Falls Pond. This is a beautiful, eight-acre pond that offers excellent opportunities for hiking, fishing and picnicking, though a series of wooden steps must be climbed to make your way to the trail. The Lovequist Loop that circles the pond is an easy walk of less than a mile, and the grade is not difficult. There are many places to stop and sit, and stunning views of the surrounding Bear and Table Mountains abound. It is, simply, a pleasant and peaceful walk through the forest, an interesting contrast to the roaring waters of the gorge just a short distance away. Though Falls Pond may be a crowded site during peak season because of its accessibility, an early morning visit will be calm and peaceful, and you might be rewarded with a view of the local wildlife.

Historical Information

Interestingly, unlike Lower Falls, Rocky Gorge has been a destination site for tourists since the 1860s, ever since White Mountain tourism got its start. In fact, the bridge that crosses the gorge today is not the first bridge at this location, as it has been replaced a number of times over 150 years or more.

As you turn right out of this scenic area and continue your journey westward, you will soon lose sight of the Swift River. While the river will remain close at hand to the right, it is out of view due to the dense forest. About three miles down the highway, you will come to the only road that joins up with the Kancamagus Highway.

Bear Notch Road

What to Know

This is the only through road that intersects with the Kancamagus Highway for its entire length. For much of its history, Bear Notch Road was a dirt road, then a gravel road, but now it is fully paved, running nine miles to the town of Bartlett. However, it remains a seasonal road that is gated off, about a mile from the Kancamagus Highway on its southern end, and closed from approximately December to mid-May, though the times do vary depending on weather conditions and maintenance concerns. I've read many comments online that question whether this road is worth the extra detour, and the answer to that question is an unqualified yes. It will add time to your trip, but it's an interesting and worthwhile diversion. If you've already traveled the entire length of the Kanc and seen all it has to offer, Bear Notch Road does junction with Route 302 in Bartlett, which can then be taken to complete a driving loop to take in even more White Mountain scenery. However, if you're a first-time visitor, and you're considering taking Bear Notch Road instead of continuing on the Kanc, you'd be missing out on a lot of scenery. Though it's an eighteen-mile round-trip detour, many visitors take the road up to Bartlett (where there is a historic covered bridge that houses an interesting gift shop), then turn around and come back down Bear Notch Road to continue on the rest of the Kanc. I've done this many times over the years, and somehow Bear Notch Road never grows old.

Points of Interest

Bear Notch is a winding road and narrower than the Kanc, and much of it runs through dense forest, crossing both the Swift River and Douglass

Rainy day mountain view looking northward from a pull-off on Bear Notch Road. *Author photo.*

Brook. There are also several overlook spots worth checking out that offer spectacular mountain views at all times of the year. The northern portion of the road runs through the Bartlett Experimental Forest. This is a Forest Service research station that was established in 1932 as a silvicultural site, and its trails and roads are open to the public. The forest can be accessed by taking Upper Haystack Road off Bear Notch Road, which serves as its southern boundary, several miles before Bartlett Village is reached. You can follow this to Loop Road, which intersects with Bear Notch Road closer to Bartlett. As to the name of this road, Bear Notch Road does in fact pass through a gap, or notch, between aptly named Bear Mountain (3,219 ft.) to the east and Bartlett Haystack Mountain (2,995 ft.) to the west. And if you're wondering about bears themselves, don't be surprised if you see a bear wandering alongside Bear Notch Road or crossing the road at certain times of the year. After all, it's their road!

Historical Information

This road has an interesting history all its own. Like the Kancamagus Highway, it runs along the approximate course of an old logging railroad, in this case the previously discussed Bartlett & Albany Railroad. Soon after the demise of that line, this road was developed as a connecting route, running nine miles between the town of Bartlett and the Passaconaway settlement.

Once you turn right back onto the Kancamagus Highway, less than a mile or so up the road, you will come to one of the main areas of settlement that once existed at Passaconaway in Albany. The home and workplace of over one thousand people at its peak in the early 1900s, Passaconaway is now all but a memory except for the Russell-Colbath House.

Russell-Colbath Historic Site

What to Know

The Russell-Colbath House, as it is known today, is the oldest of the man-made features to be found along the Kancamagus Highway. At first glance, it might not look impressive, as there are no scenic views of the Swift River immediately visible. However, it is a site well worth visiting to learn about the people who once called this area home and the railroad activities that once took place here. There is ample parking at the site, which once served as an official visitor center, and a pass is required. The walk to the historic house is an easy one, approximately one hundred yards, and there are modern restroom facilities. It is open from Memorial Day through Columbus Day, though visitors can easily access the grounds out of season, if it hasn't snowed too much. The Russell-Colbath House is also open for guided tours and historic demonstrations in July and August, but hours and times may vary so, it is advised to call the Saco River Ranger Station (603 447 5448) for more details or up-to-date information.

Points of Interest

On this site, one will find, in addition to the historic house, a modern barn (there was an original barn that survived into the twentieth century

The Russell-Colbath House circa 1961, when it was first used as a visitor center on the Kancamagus Highway. *National Archives, courtesy Forest History Society.*

and was later taken down) built in 2003 that sometimes offers public demonstrations and two historic cemeteries. Just a short distance away from the house and barn is the entry path to the Rail and River Trail. With its gravel path and wooden bridges, this half-mile walking trail is accessible to people with disabilities and details the interesting history of the area. Right at this location, the Swift River Railroad ran along the river and behind the Russell-Colbath House; there was a railroad switch and siding, a number of railroad buildings and a general store for locals and loggers alike that was first operated by the Russell family. Needless to say, there was a lot of activity in this area, and while few remnants survive, interpretative signs have been placed to help to tell the story of the olden days here. The walk is a quick, easy and enjoyable one that offers a view of the river, while the size of some of the downed trees along the path is quite impressive. There are also picnic tables and benches near the Russell-Colbath House for the convenience of visitors.

Historic Information

The house itself, as historians Justine Gringas and David Ruell have documented, is important as it "stands as the only remaining example of the nineteenth century farmstead occupancy of the Passaconaway Valley." Built from 1831 to 1832 by Thomas Russell and his sons and later acquired by his son Amzi, it remains largely unaltered, except for some changes to its parlor made from 1860 to 1861. This "modernization" was inspired, according to tradition, by Eliza George Russell, Amzi's wife, after her visit to a wealthy sea captain's home. Interestingly, because of the George family's association with the land and some confusion about the house itself (some believing it was the original house built by Austin George), it is often referred to in records incorrectly as the George house. The home is a center-chimney, one-and-a-half story farm Cape house, a typical nineteenth-century style that differed from the older Cape-style homes of New England by being "somewhat taller." Visitors will note the wide floorboards, all from local, old-growth timber; the old kitchen with its large beehive oven (a modern kitchen was later added); the old paneled doors with Norfolk latches only; and the wide-board wainscoting. The only heat in the house comes from the big fireplace, while running water and the new bathroom at the rear were only added in 1948. The water originally came from a well just outside the front door. As historians Gingras and Ruell note, "From the time it was built in 1831, George House has always been associated with the changing use of the valley land—from pioneer settlement, to farming and lumbering, to seasonal recreation use." As the panels on the front door show, this house also served as the Passaconaway Post Office from 1892 to 1906, with Priscilla Russell Colbath serving as postmistress. Though I have given her life story in a previous chapter, it is worth reiterating that Priscilla Colbath was born in this house and lived most of her life here, the last twenty-five years alone, before dying in 1930. She was, in fact, one of the last year-round residents of Passaconaway, which had faded away to a ghost town. After Colbath's death, the house was used as a summer residence until it was purchased by the U.S. Forest Service in 1961.

Not far from the Russell-Colbath House will be found two historic cemeteries on the property. The oldest one, closest to the house, began as the family cemetery for the George family, the first settlers in Passaconaway, whose home was located just a short distance away. Plain fieldstone grave markers are located near the entrance on the left for members of that

The Russell-Colbath House was built in 1832 and is the oldest man-made structure on the Kancamagus Highway. *Author photo.*

family. The same is true for the members of the Russell family buried here; only Priscilla Russell Colbath has an inscribed stone. In this rural location, where everyone knew each other, there was no need to mark the names of the deceased on their gravestones at first, as the family knew who was buried where; they weren't thinking about posterity or future generations of genealogists. Over the years, as the area gained more residents, this cemetery evolved, as was common in New England, from a family cemetery into a community cemetery that was open to all who lived here, including summer residents. Renowned hunter and guide Jack Allen (1835–1912) is buried here, as are early settlers Thomas Shackford (1800–1864), whose son operated a famed hotel in Passaconaway, and Benjamin Swinston (1865–1939), a New York native and caretaker and close friend to Priscilla Colbath and the last of the year-round residents of Passaconaway. Among the modern burial sites here is that of Edward McKenzie (1925–2012), who served as a ball-turret gunner aboard a B-17 Flying Fortress bomber, was shot down on his fifth mission over Germany and survived as a POW for over a year before returning home. The second

The grave marker for Ruth Priscilla Russell Colbath. She left a candle in the window of her home for decades while awaiting her husband's return. *Author photo.*

cemetery, while often classified as part of the Passaconaway Cemetery, is actually a separate family cemetery for the Burbank and Mayhew families; James Mayhew (1840–95) came to the area about 1870 and established the Carrigain House hotel. He was a native of England who came here as a young man. When the Civil War broke out in 1861, he was living in Barnston, Quebec, and enlisted for service from Conway with the soon-to-be-famed Second New Hampshire Regiment of Volunteers. Mayhew was wounded in action at the Second Battle of Bull Run in August 1862 but lived to tell the tale and continued his service after recuperating for over a year. He likely had some interesting stories to entertain his hotel guests. This cemetery, with its high granite walls and fancy wrought-iron gate, clearly shows that these families wanted a space all their own.

As you turn right out of the Russell-Colbath Historic Site, the last of the designated historic or scenic sites on the highway located in the town of Albany, you are now traveling through the remainder of the area of Passaconaway and into Waterville Valley. You'll see the sign for Sabbaday Falls about 2.9 miles down the highway on the left.

At this point, you have now journeyed 15.4 miles from Conway, reaching almost the halfway point on the Kancamagus Highway.

SABBADAY FALLS OBSERVATION SITE

What to Know

Sabbaday Falls is one of the most visited waterfalls in the state of New Hampshire, making this site one of the most popular along the Kanc. That's not surprising, as it offers the opportunity to see a spectacular and charming waterfall in a relatively easy fashion. The site does require a pass, and there is a parking lot that holds about forty vehicles. However, in peak season the parking lot is often full. In the parking lot there are simple restroom facilities, and at the beginning of the trail there are picnic tables available, as well as interpretive panels that tell the history of the waterfall and the beginning of the tourist trade. The trail along Sabbaday Brook to the falls is wide and very compacted and smoothly graded, without rocks or roots; the whole hike to and from the falls is about .7 miles. Online website descriptions regarding the ease of this trail for all are somewhat misleading in my estimation, though it is rated as one of the trails along the Kanc that is compliant with the Americans with Disabilities Act (ADA). While the trail itself is easy and excellently maintained, it does rise in elevation and becomes steeper as you get closer to the falls. If you're a hiker or someone in good physical condition, the trek will be no problem. However, for young children who tire easily, those in lesser physical condition or the disabled, especially those in a wheelchair, it will be more daunting. My petite adult daughter in a wheelchair was able to make it to the falls but only with the aid of myself and her able-bodied uncle pushing and pulling her wheelchair uphill. That being said, there are benches along the length of the trail where one can sit for a spell and catch your breath if needed, and they offer wonderful views of the brook that are well worth the walk, even if you can't make it all the way up. As you approach the falls, there are two different trails to take. The main trail continues straight to the upper falls, but the one off to the left takes you down to the base of the falls, including the wonderful lower pool into which it cascades. The water here is so clear, one wishes that it was possible to take a swim here, but alas, swimming is prohibited at Sabbaday Falls. However, wading in the brook five hundred feet above and below the falls is allowed. From the pool, walkways will bring you to the top of the Sabbaday Falls, so this is certainly the best course to follow for the finest viewing experience. Visitors, of course, are reminded to stay on the walkways, and climbing on the rail, for fun or a better picture of the waterfall, should be avoided for safety reasons. It should be noted that while the Sabbaday Brook Trail is

Upper level of Sabbaday Falls. *Author photo.*

open year-round, the walkways nearest to the falls are closed to visitors and gated off to prevent access from November through about mid-May. This can be a disappointment for visitors making the trip here late in the fall season before the snow sets in, so plan accordingly.

Points of Interest

Interpretive panels on this trail tell the fascinating story of the formation of this waterfall over the course of some ten thousand years and the different geological processes involved. The pool is impressive for its high sides, an indication of how much rock the water has carved through over the ages, and for its clear water. As you walk the steps along the course of the falls to reach the top, you will note that the falls, which drops about forty feet in all (some accounts give the drop as thirty-five feet, others forty-five feet), does so in several stages. One section of the walkway goes over the second stage of the falls where it makes a sharp turn to the right, and on a hot summer day the temperature here is notably cooler due to water vapor that emanates from the roiling water below. Very cool, in more ways than one. At peak times, there are many visitors here, but with time, perseverance and patience, excellent photographic shots of the falls can be had. Once you reach the top, there is a nice viewing platform of the falls that gives one a different and equally enchanting view. As one geologist, quoted in the *White Mountain Guide* in 1881, stated, the features of Sabbaday Falls "all combine to form a picture of beauty, which, once fixed in the mind, is a joy forever." Once at the top of the falls, the Sabbaday Brook Trail does not end here. For those wishing to make a day of hiking, this trail continues for another five and a half miles to the summits of two 4,000-footers, Middle Tripyramid (4,110 ft.) and North Tripyramid (4,140 ft.) Mountains. This difficult hike is covered in chapter 8.

Historical Information

Nearly as interesting as Sabbaday Falls is the human history that surrounds the site. Two local legends speak to how the falls gained its name. One states that when settlers first came into the area around Passaconaway in the 1790s, they made a stop near the falls on the Sabbath Day (Sunday) in order to rest. However, once they saw the remote conditions in which they would be living, they turned around and went back home. The most accepted legend regarding the naming of the falls states that road builders working in the area late in the season, probably in the 1830s or 1840s, laid their tools down on a Saturday and headed home the next day, Sunday, naming the brook and falls before they departed. Intending to come back the next spring to finish their work, they never did. The name today, Sabbaday Falls, is simply a corrupted version, likely representative of the local dialect, of Sabbath Day. Both legends probably have a basis in factual events, for as I've recounted, the first settlers in the 1790s and early 1800s in this area did not last long and did indeed return home. As to the road workers, it is also true that Passaconaway and Sabbaday Falls does mark the western limit of the road from Conway into Albany, and as I've also recounted, the section of the road west from Passaconaway to Lincoln was actually the last section of the Kancamagus Highway to be completed—but over 150 years after the falls was first discovered. Perhaps one day that stash of workers' road-building tools will be discovered to corroborate the legend. Finally, in regard to the naming of the falls, one other name was also applied to it by guidebook editor Moses Sweetser in the late nineteenth century. In his White Mountain guidebook, he refers to the site as Church's Falls, naming it after the well-known American landscape painter Frederick E. Church. Sweetser wrote that the falls "have been visited and painted by F.E. Church." This artist, who was famed in his day as one of America's greatest painters, was a native of Connecticut and a student of famed landscape artist Thomas Cole, who also visited the White Mountains and painted some notable works, including one depicting Mount Chocorua. Church painted in northern New England at times from the 1850s to the 1860s, but Sabbaday Falls does not seem to have been the subject of any of his finished oil paintings. However, Church also executed thousands of sketches during the course of his career, and it is likely the work he did at Sabbaday Falls was one of these. It's possible that such a sketch was perhaps used as a study for another of his finished works, as his New Hampshire landscapes were largely composites, rather than paintings of any one location. Church was just one of many landscape painters who came to the White Mountains and became a part of the White Mountain School of painters, which began with Thomas Cole's visit in 1827 and continued into the 1900s. Had Frederick Church's painting become a famous one, like a number of his other works, it is possible the name Church's Falls might have stuck, but it was not to be, and the name of the falls, rightfully so, has reverted to that dictated by local tradition and legend.

One part of Sabbaday Falls's history that is fact is its association with the Passaconaway House hotel, owned and operated by James Shackford. It was located just a short distance from here toward Conway, and the falls was a nearby attraction frequented by its guests from the 1870s until the hotel's demise in the second decade of the 1900s. In fact, it was James Shackford who cut the current Sabbaday Brook Trail in 1880. He did so on behalf of the Appalachian Mountain Club (AMC), for which he worked on the side, serving as a guide and blazing trails. Perhaps unfamiliar to many today, the AMC, America's oldest outdoors organization, was established in Massachusetts in 1876 by academics from the Massachusetts Institute of Technology and some wealthy individuals with vacation interests in New Hampshire. Their first goals were to publish accurate maps of the White Mountains, gather scientific data and preserve the natural beauty and the history of the area. The AMC has accomplished much in the White Mountains and many other locations outside New Hampshire over the years, the Sabbaday Brook Trail being among their many early initiatives.

As you depart Sabbaday Falls and continue your trip on the Kancamagus Highway westward, you are now beginning the second phase of the journey. From here on out, though the Swift River is not far away, at least for a little while, it remains out of sight, and the focus is no longer on views of this river or historical sites but rather on spectacular mountain views. Now, the Kanc begins its rises in elevation as it winds toward Kancamagus Pass, but there are several sites to see before you get there; your next stopping point is in 1.9 miles.

SUGAR HILL SCENIC VISTA OVERLOOK

What to Know

Located about two miles west of Sabbaday Falls, this scenic spot is the first of several overlooks encountered from the east that have been established on the western end of the Kancamagus Highway. The parking lot requires no pass and is large, but there are no restroom facilities here. There is a pavilion that offers shade and interpretive sign panels that give information as to the surrounding view. Please note that while the Sugar Hill Overlook is not gated off in the off-season, visitors should beware that during the snowy months, the parking lot is not plowed or maintained and is not accessible.

Points of Interest

The Sugar Hill Overlook offers a gorgeous view of the Swift River valley and the mountains in the area. Prime among them, of course, is Sugar Hill (1,840 ft.), just over a mile in the distance, whose name comes from the sugar maple trees that are found there in abundance. This is also a common name in the state, with nine eminences throughout northern New Hampshire bearing this name. Farther off in the distance are Birch Hill (1,888 ft.), named after the many birch trees in the area, and Greens Cliff (2,926 ft.), Owl Cliff (2,950 ft.) and Mount Tremont (3,950 ft.) even farther off to the left. Greens Cliff, which is not accessible from the Kancamagus, is an interesting and now popular climbing spot, its main wall, featuring a band of white rock, clearly visible even at this distance. This cliff once was easily accessible during the old logging days, when there was a system of trails, but once the industry faded, so, too, did these trails. A band of AMC hikers tried to scale the cliff in the fall of 1928 but could only ascend 100 feet before being forced to turn back. Following this, its remote location left Greens Cliff largely forgotten, and it was not until the late 1970s that attention on the cliffs came into focus again. However, according to writer Josh Laskin, it would not be until the late 1990s and early 2000s that new routes to scale Greens Cliff began to be fully developed. Today, the climbing at Greens Cliff, with some sixty-five routes, is said to "rival the best at Cathedral Ledge" in Conway, and according to experienced climber Ray Rice, "It's some of the last remaining pristine granite in New Hampshire." The views at this spot are wonderful at all times of the year but are excellent in the fall season; the many maple trees present a flaming red color alongside many other hues, signature features that draw thousands of visitors here every year.

Continuing right out of the parking lot and continuing on your journey west toward Lincoln, the next site of interest is two miles ahead on the right. Be sure to look carefully, as the sign for Lily Pond is easily missed.

LILY POND VISTA

What to Know

This small mountain pond offers some of the most pleasant scenery to be found along the Kancamagus Highway, but it is probably one of the least visited and most overlooked. This occurs for several reasons. First, there is only a simple wooden sign for Lily Pond, so it is easy to miss, as is the pond itself when the leaves are on the trees. Second, there is no parking lot for the site, just a pull-off that will hold maybe eight to ten vehicles parked parallel with the road, though there is enough space farther down the highway for additional parking if you're willing to walk farther. In short, if you're new to driving the Kanc, unless you've read this or other guides, you're likely just to drive on by, blissfully unaware of what there is to see. Access to the shoreline is available via several small, narrow paths from the pull-off. These paths do go downhill and are not accessible for people with disabilities, but the going is fairly manageable for many. Closer to the pond, you may encounter some muddy areas, so plan accordingly, depending on the season. However, even if you cannot make it down to the shore, the views from the road are still worth a stop at all times of the year. There are no benches or places to sit at Lily Pond, so if you want to stay for a while, and you may very well want to, bring your own camp chair.

Points of Interest

This high mountain pond, with an elevation of 2,060 feet, used to be in a remote location and seldom saw human visitors, but this changed with the building of the highway in the 1950s. Lily Pond is but four acres in size and is only 4 or 5 feet deep at most times of the year. The views of the pond are so pleasing and the place so quiet that it's hard to believe the highway is just 100 feet or so away. The vista across the pond and off in the distance is amazing and one of my favorites along the whole highway, especially during the fall season. Serving as a backdrop for the pond looking northward is Mount Carrigain (4,700 ft.) and a spur of Mount Huntington (3,680 ft.). On a sunny day, excellent photographic opportunities abound, the water offering nice reflective views of the surrounding mountains and coniferous trees. While there is no trail around the pond, if you don't mind getting a bit wet, you can make your way partway around the pond on the white rocks that abound on its shore. Though small, the pond, with its water vegetation, offers an excellent opportunity to see some wild animals, including several species of birds, ducks and, most importantly, an occasional moose if you visit at the right time. Additionally, since the pond is stocked with brown trout, it does serve as a quiet fishing spot and also offers an opportunity for kayakers. While Lily Pond is not an extensive or challenging kayaking destination, heading out on the waters offers some rewarding views, including North Tripyramid Mountain (4,160 ft.) to the south of the Kancamagus Highway, and the possibility of seeing the local wildlife in an even closer setting. It is true that there are other, larger ponds that are accessible from trails alongside the Kancamagus, but none offers the nonhiker the experience of this interesting mountain ecosystem in such a quick and easy fashion as does Lily Pond.

Once you depart Lily Pond heading westward, the highway continues its winding course as it heads toward the C.L. Graham Wangan Overlook and Kancamagus Pass 2.4 miles ahead. The scenery off to the right (north) on this section of the highway, which narrows at times, becomes spectacular, offering exhilarating mountain views that please at all times of the year. Drivers should pay close attention to the road on this section, as it is possible to be distracted by the scenery.

C.L. Graham Wangan Overlook

What to Know

This overlook, the last of the north-facing scenic sites directly on the Kancamagus Highway, is a popular spot, offering spectacular views of the surrounding mountains. The site hosts many visitors during peak times, but its parking lot, which requires no pass, is large enough to accommodate many cars and trucks, as well as recreational vehicles and tour buses. There are no restroom facilities, though there is a pavilion that offers shade and some interpretive signs. These explain the view of the Swift River watershed, the overlook being very close—within a mile—to the headwaters of the Swift River and even closer to Kancamagus Pass just up the highway. In addition to the main parking lot on the north side of the highway, there is an upper parking lot on the opposite side of the highway that also has many spaces and, during peak times, is often more accessible to those approaching this overlook from Lincoln to the west. During the busiest times on weekends in the fall season, there are so many people here that the atmosphere is downright festive. Don't be surprised if you find artists or craftspeople who have set up shop here to sell their creations, offering an excellent opportunity to purchase a unique souvenir of your visit. At other times you may happen on a marriage proposal or engagement ceremony being conducted, and why not? It's a beautiful setting to begin a life together. While the overlook can become crowded, don't despair, as there is space enough for all to get some impressive photos with a little patience. For a full viewing experience, be sure to check out the vista from the upper parking lot for a more distant perspective. It's worth the effort. The C.L. Graham Wangan Overlook is not gated off during the off-season, but it is not maintained in the winter. However, it is often partially plowed and more accessible than other overlooks on the Kanc, but don't expect this always to be the case.

Points of Interest

As you look northward from the pavilion or the rock wall to the side, you're viewing the beginnings of the Swift River, with Mount Huntington (3,730 ft.) in the distance to the left and Mount Hancock (4,430 ft.) and Mount Hancock East Peak (4,035 ft.) even farther off in the distance beyond the Swift and Sawyer Rivers (which are not visible). The view is simply stunning in the fall, with a wide range of colors. A visit here even outside the fall season is worthwhile, whether it's on an early winter's day before the snow has come or in the spring before the trees have come into full bloom. Early morning visits before or near sunrise or at sunset can also be spectacular, with the added views of the moon and, perhaps, of headlights off in the distance to the right as cars make their twisting and turning approach toward Kancamagus Pass. However, the late afternoon and early evening, when the sun is at your back, are the best times for photographers. At quiet times before sunrise or after sunset, while taking shelter in the pavilion, you may even be reminded by the local wildlife that this area is indeed a remote one, even if the drive to Lincoln is but short. Perhaps you'll see a deer or a moose during the fall rutting season or maybe even hear a moose bellow while in search of a mate. All of these experiences are possible here if your timing is good and you have a bit of luck.

Historical Information

This overlook honors two facets of White Mountain history. Clifford L. Graham (1894–1954) was a native of Minneapolis, Minnesota, with New Hampshire roots, moving here as a young man. He studied forestry at the University of New Hampshire and Yale University and, fittingly, first worked as a forest guard in the Swift River valley and later as a ranger in the Twin Mountain District. He was working as forest supervisor at the Cumberland

National Forest prior to being appointed forest supervisor of the White Mountain National Forest in June 1936. The sixth man to hold this position, he knew the area of the Kancamagus Highway well, and his tenure was one of the longest, lasting until his death in 1954. Much of the Kancamagus Highway was constructed during his tenure. In contrast, the word *Wangan* in this overlook's name speaks to the logging activities that once took place here. The term is an Algonquian one, a Wangan ground being a meeting place. However, the term *wangan* would later be adopted by men working in the lumber industry. It was used by them to designate a place for storing lumber camp supplies, as well as a forest commissary, where lumbermen could purchase shoes, clothing, tobacco and other supplies for their personal use. This is the context of its use in the name for this overlook, according to Sarah Jordan, the heritage program manager and forest archaeologist for the White Mountain National Forest.

As you turn right out of the main parking lot (or left out of the upper lot) to continue the trip westward, the Kancamagus Highway climbs the last tenth of a mile to its highest elevation, the steepest part of the drive. This stretch of road, completed in 1959, was the most difficult and challenging to construct. As you approach Kancamagus Pass, you will see its sign in the distance and can now look for a safe spot along the road to park.

Kancamagus Pass

What to Know

The physical location of Kancamagus Pass is denoted by a prominent roadside sign. Though this is not an official scenic spot, and there is no parking lot, there is ample space for parking alongside and well off the highway safely on both sides. However, visitors should remain cautious and, if they have to do so, be very careful when crossing the road. If the highway is crowded during your visit, and you don't mind a short uphill walk, it will be safer to park in the parking lot for Pemigewasset Overlook (see next section).

Sign at Kancamagus Pass, with the mountain in the background. *Author photo.*

Points of Interest

Many visitors stop at this, the highest point on the mountainous Kancamagus Highway and take pictures with the sign or Mount Kancamagus (3,700 ft.) in the background. That mountain is on the south side of the highway, looking back the way you came as you're heading west, while straight ahead, heading toward Lincoln, is the silhouette of Mount Hitchcock (3,648 ft.) in the distance. In fact, the pass also serves as the town boundary line between Livermore and Lincoln. While enjoying the view, consider the fact that you have been traveling on one of the highest roads to be found in all of New England. While the nearby Mount Washington Auto Road, with an elevation of 6,286 feet, tops them all, the Kancamagus Highway, which here reaches an elevation of 2,855 feet, is in the top five. It is interesting to note that all the higher mountain roads—the Mount Washington Auto Road and those leading to the tops of Mount Mansfield (3,850 ft.) and Mount Equinox (3,840 ft.) in Vermont and Mount Greylock (3,491 ft.) in Massachusetts— are only open seasonally, require a fee and have limitations as to what kind of vehicles can travel on them. Only the Kancamagus Highway, which is longer than all of them by far, is open year-round, is toll-free and has no major vehicle restrictions. The highway may have taken over 120 years to come to fruition, but in its final version, it was made to be shared by all, both locals and visitors alike, all year long.

As you pull away from Kancamagus Pass, exercise care when rejoining the highway. Your next scenic spot, Pemigewasset Overlook, is just a tenth of a mile down the road on the left and can be easily missed.

PEMIGEWASSET OVERLOOK

What to Know

This overlook is the first of several spectacular vistas of the Osceola Range and the East Branch Pemigewasset River valley that are found as you travel from east to west on the Kancamagus Highway. The parking lot here is a large one that can accommodate larger vehicles and requires no pass. However, it is not plowed or maintained in the off-season. There are restroom facilities here, though they are not accessible for people with disabilities. A short downhill walk, about one hundred yards, is required to reach the viewing area, which has a pavilion and interpretive signing. With all its open space, it's a nice place to gather for a summer or fall picnic. While the overlook is spectacular at all times of the year, it is especially so in the fall. Given the overlook's westward-facing orientation, this is an excellent place for stunning sunset photographic views, so plan accordingly if this is your goal.

Points of Interest

It is at this overlook, the newest of those created along the Kanc, that the focus of the highway's scenic sites turns to the south and west. Now that you've left the Swift River behind, a new watershed, that of the East Branch Pemigewasset River, comes to the forefront. Though you may not realize it, this small river, which is just under sixteen miles long, is an important one and part of one of New England's most historic watersheds. The East Branch gets its start in northeastern Lincoln near Mount Carrigain (4,647 ft.) and flows south and west to meet up with the Pemigewasset River in North Woodstock.

From here, the "Pemi," as it is called by locals, soon becomes part of the larger Merrimack River watershed via the Winnipesaukee River. The Merrimack River—which was once claimed by the Massachusetts Bay Colony as its territorial boundary, resulting in a border dispute with New Hampshire that began in the 1640s and lasted one hundred years—flows south through New Hampshire and Massachusetts before emptying into the Atlantic Ocean at Newburyport. Indeed, if you're visiting the Kanc from Boston, anywhere in southern New England or New York and beyond, you've crossed this river or its tributaries, perhaps without giving it a thought. What a difference a few miles can make when it comes to water flow. The Swift River, as you know by now, has its beginnings just a short distance away from here, but it flows in a different direction, heading eastward and emptying into the Saco River at Conway. The Saco River then continues its course to the Atlantic Ocean, reaching its destination on the Maine coast, some sixty miles north of the mouth of the Merrimack River in Newburyport. As to the views at this overlook, the sign panels give excellent information as to what you're seeing of the Osceola Mountains, which are part of the Sandwich Range, and beyond.

Sunset view of the Osceola Range at the Pemigewasset Overlook. *Author photo.*

From left to right, your first point of interest here is Osceola Mountain East Peak (4,156 ft.), whose "ragged profile," as the sign states, was "plucked by a glacier" millions of years ago. Next comes Mount Osceola (4,340 ft.), named after a famed Seminole chief. It once had a fire observation tower at its summit. Continuing on, there is visible Osceola Mountain Middle Peak (4,240 ft.), followed by Osceola Mountain West Peak (4,114 ft.). The first two of the Osceola Mountains mentioned above are part of New Hampshire's famed group of "4,000-footer" mountain peaks (there are forty-eight in all). To climb every one of them is the goal of countless hikers in New England and beyond. Continuing on with the panoramic view, East Scar Ridge (3,793 ft.) is next and, finally, far off in the distance are Mount Wolf (3,448 ft.) in Lincoln and Black Mountain (2,930 ft.) in Benton. Interestingly, Scar Ridge lives up to its name and is a difficult climb for some hikers, while Mount Wolf is accessible via the Appalachian Trail and is also known for one of its features, Dilly Cliff, the site of a devastating forest fire in 2017.

Turn left out of the parking lot to continue west toward the town of Lincoln. Your next must-see destination, the Hancock Overlook, is 1.9 miles ahead on the left. However, before you arrive here, there is an unnamed lookout 1.4 miles distant on the left that is also worth stopping at, if traffic conditions in this direction allow. Though it is best accessed when traveling eastward, this simple gravel pull-off that holds four or five cars offers a great view of Mount Osceola.

HANCOCK OVERLOOK

What to Know

This overlook is the last of the scenic overlook viewpoints directly on the Kanc as you travel from Conway to Lincoln. No parking pass is required here, though buses, RVs and vehicles with trailers are prohibited due to the tight nature of its location. The parking lot is kept partially clear throughout the year. There is a pavilion that provides shade, in which interpretive signs discuss the view and New Hampshire mountain climbing in general. There are no restroom facilities. This parking lot also serves as a starting point for the Hancock Notch Trail. Because of its location on the hairpin turn, exiting the Hancock Overlook should be done with extreme care.

View from the Hancock Overlook at the hairpin turn. The highway, barely visible at far right, runs just below the line of trees in the foreground. *Author photo.*

Points of Interest

The view here, also a must-see, offers another stunning vantage point looking southwest at the Osceola Mountains. Osceola Mountain East Peak is at far left (obscured by trees much of the year) as you look out from the pavilion, followed by Osceola Mountain Middle and West Peaks as you look to the right. At the far right is East Scar Ridge, whose peak is more rounded than those of the Osceolas. As you look at these mountains, you cannot help but notice the slide scars on the slopes. These scars are long and narrow exposures of the mountain bedrock that formed over many years when debris scoured the soil and regolith on top of the underlying rock due to rain and melting snow action. They are visible in the summer and can look like small rivers flowing downward but are more easily distinguishable in the wintertime by the snow and ice that gathers in their crevices. This overlook is also interesting due to its location at the famed hairpin turn on the Kancamagus Highway. Looking below the Osceola Mountains from the pavilion, or from the rock wall lining the parking

Close-up view of the Osceola Range from Hancock Overlook. *Author photo.*

Winter view of the slide scars on the Osceola Mountains from the Hancock Overlook. *Author photo.*

Fall view of Lower Falls and pool below. A perfect place to swim. *Author photo.*

Close-up view of Lower Falls. *Author photo.*

Left: View of Rocky Gorge looking northward. Note the deeply cut channel. *Author photo*.

Below: Fall view of the two cemeteries adjacent to the Russell-Colbath House. The oldest graves here date to the late 1700s. *Author photo*.

Summer view of the footbridge over Rocky Gorge looking downstream on the Swift River.
Dan Hanscom, Shutterstock.

Sabbaday Falls, White Mountains, N.H.

Left: Postcard view of Sabbaday Falls, circa 1900. *Author collection.*

Below: The lower pool at Sabbaday Falls. Note the clear water and the towering rock wall. *Author photo.*

Fall view of the Sugar Hill overlook. *Author photo.*

Aerial view of the Kancamagus Highway near Sugar Hill. *Wangkun Jia, Shutterstock.*

Mountain scenery at the Sugar Hill Scenic Overlook. *Author photo*.

Lily Pond vista looking north. A good place to watch for moose. *Author photo*.

Reflective view of east end, Lily Pond. *Author photo.*

A fall view of the mountain scenery at the C.L. Graham Wangan Overlook. *Author photo.*

View from the upper parking lot, C.L. Graham Wangan Overlook. Even when the leaves are gone, the Kancamagus Highway affords beautiful scenery. *Author photo.*

Sunset view of the Kancamagus Pass. *Jon Bilous, Shutterstock.*

Winter sunset view at Pemigewasset Overlook. *Author photo.*

The Osceola Range from an unnamed overlook on the Kancamagus Highway. *Author photo.*

An aerial view of the hairpin turn and Hancock Overlook. *Wangkun Jia, Shutterstock.*

View of lower Otter Falls. A great place to swim. *Author photo.*

View of the East Pemigewasset River looking northward. *Author photo.*

A young male moose feeding in Church Pond near the Kancamagus Highway. *Carolyn Pelkey Photography, Shutterstock.*

A black bear (*Ursus americanus*) in the White Mountains. *C.R. Maloney, Shutterstock.*

View of green ice on the lower Swift River. *Author photo.*

Late fall view of Champney Falls. *Courtesy Rebecca Coleman.*

View of Pitcher Falls, close by Champney Falls and just off the Champney Brook Trail. *Courtesy Rebecca Coleman.*

Aerial view, Kancamagus Highway and the town of Lincoln. The mountains of the Osceola Range are in the background. *Wangkun Jia, Shutterstock.*

Aerial view westward from Pemigewasset Overlook. *Wangkun Jia, Shutterstock.*

Open-road view of the Kancamagus Highway in the fall. *Author photo.*

View around the hairpin turn traveling eastward, with mountains looming in the distance. *Author photo.*

lot, you can see the highway as it curves below. Go to the north side of the parking lot, and you can see the outcropping of granite rock through which this section of the highway was cut. Interestingly, though the site is now heavily wooded, when the highway was first completed, the overlook and surrounding area were largely devoid of trees.

Turn left out of the Hancock Overlook to continue your trip toward the town of Lincoln. The hairpin turn used here was designed to lessen the grade of the road as you ascend or descend near Kancamagus Pass. The Otter Rocks site, your next destination, is 3.2 miles ahead on the left. The views on this section of the highway are not as interesting, but occasionally you can catch a glimpse of the Hancock Branch, which parallels the highway off to the left.

Otter Rocks Day Use Area

What to Know

This is a popular swimming destination in the summertime, and its parking lot, which requires a pass, often fills up quite early. Access to the pleasant waters of the Hancock Branch is not too difficult for most people, but I would not consider the area accessible to people with disabilities, especially those who use wheelchairs. Picnic tables are available, as are bathroom facilities, but these are also not fully accessible to people with disabilities. The swimming here is especially suitable for young children, unless the stream is at a high-water stage. Because of the natural beauty of this site, a stop here is recommended even if you don't plan to take a swim.

Points of Interest

This area is one of the most charming of the water sites along the Kancamagus Highway. Here at Otter Rocks, the waters of the Hancock Branch cascade gently over the rocks, creating small pools along the way and one larger main pool. The water at most times of the year is fairly shallow, with the main pool averaging about four feet deep. There are many flat rocks on which to sit and enjoy the view or catch some sun before or after swimming, while the tree-lined banks nearby offer plenty of shade.

Turn left out of Otter Rocks as you continue westward. The Forest Discovery Trail is just .8 miles ahead on your right.

Forest Discovery Trail

What to Know

There is plenty of parking at this site, and no pass is required. Public restroom facilities are available, and they are accessible to people with disabilities. The trail here is a short, 1.5-mile loop, with only a slight elevation. It is wide and well graded and graveled and is rated as ADA-compliant. However, there is one section that has a steeper grade, and those using a wheelchair will require assistance. Not only are there interpretive signs, with ten stops that share information about the forest ecology, but there are also plenty of benches along the way. Be sure to utilize the excellent trail guide booklet which describes even more fully what the visitor can see here. Because of the nature of this site, it is a popular one for school field trips, so it's possible that when visiting in the spring or fall seasons on a weekday, you may encounter large groups. The Forest Service does have available a grade 5–8 curriculum guide online at https://www.fs.usda.gov/Internet/FSE_DOCUMENTS/ stelprdb5262259.pdf for the convenience of teachers and educators.

Points of Interest

This trail offers one of the most family-friendly and easy hikes to be found along the Kancamagus Highway. The markers along the way help you keep track of your progress, which is helpful for small children, and the trail crosses a small stream several times. The trail guide details the different "life zones" of a northern New England forest to be seen here, from the forest floor below to the "emergent" layer above the canopy of trees. If so inclined, you'll learn about such things as the "strange" hobblebush plant, the Bear Tree and many other aspects of the forest while on your walk. The views are beautiful, and you will gain a new perspective on this important habitat.

Historical Information

The trail guide and interpretive signage also speak to the historical nature of this area and the impact of human activity. Part of the trail here runs along the old bed of a logging railroad, and near sign no. 4 you will see off to your left the mounds that were created by loggers who built the railroad that was used here to get the timber out. This area was heavily logged for years, and many logging camps were once found in the vicinity from the 1880s well into the 1920s.

Turn right out of the Forest Discovery Trail lot and follow the Kancamagus Highway to the next site, Lincoln Woods, which is 2.2 miles on the right, past the Big Rock Campground.

Lincoln Woods Visitor Center

What to Know

This site has a very large parking lot suitable for vehicles of all types, and a pass is required. There are also upgraded restroom facilities available, as well as potable water. This area is a popular one and is considered the gateway to the Pemigewasset Wilderness, being the starting point for hikes to backcountry sites like Franconia Falls and Mount Bond (4,698 ft.) and Bondcliff Mountain (4,265 ft.), to be discussed in chapter 8. There is a log cabin on the site that is sometimes opened to visitors and is staffed by the men and women of the Pemigewasset Ranger District. However, it is not manned daily at all times of the year. From the parking lot there are two ways to access bridges over the Pemigewasset River. One involves a short walk back to the Kancamagus Highway, where a sidewalk takes you to the bridge over the Pemi. There is also a more scenic view up the Pemi River from a suspension bridge that is located just below the ranger station. However, this path involves some steep steps and is not accessible to people with disabilities.

Points of Interest

It is at this point along the Kanc that the East Branch Pemigewasset River coming from the north meets up with the Hancock Branch; the East Branch flows several more miles farther southwest until it meets with the main Pemigewasset River. Both bridges here offer spectacular views northward into the Pemigewasset Wilderness, a forty-five-thousand-acre federally designated site that is the largest of its type in New Hampshire. The mountains found here are part of the Bond Range and include eight four-thousand-footers, including the two mentioned above.

Historical Information

As you visit this site today, the wilderness appears pristine, but it was not always so. This area was heavily logged out just one hundred years ago, when the area was crisscrossed by New England's largest logging railroad and the site of numerous logging camps. The timber here was transported

Suspension footbridge across the East Pemigewasset River at Lincoln Woods. *Author photo.*

to sawmills and paper mills just a few miles from here in Lincoln. Though the land here was once scarred, it has made an amazing recovery and is now fully protected.

As you make a right turn exiting here back onto the Kancamagus Highway, you are now traveling the last 2.5 miles of wilderness before coming to Loon Mountain Resort and the town of Lincoln. Along the way, the road closely parallels the East Branch Pemigewasset River on the left, of which you can get an occasional glimpse.

Loon Mountain Resort

What to Know

This well-known destination resort is located just a short distance from Interstate 93 and is one of the most easily accessible ski resorts in all of New England. It is open at all seasons of the year, and its facilities include the Kancamagus 8, an eight-seat chairlift which is billed as the most technically advanced lift of its kind in the world. With 370 skiable acres, over sixty trails and ten chairlifts, it can well accommodate its many visitors. For those visiting in the summer and fall before the snow flies, the resort offers downhill biking, gondola rides and a 750-foot zipline across the East Branch Pemi. The resort also operates a historic steam train during the winter months. For more information and up-to-date details, please go to https://www.loonmtn.com/.

Historical Information

Even if you're just passing by on your journey along the Kanc, it's worth making a stop to check out the historic locomotive that is easily visible from the highway. This is the Porter No. 3, a fifty-ton saddle tank engine that was built in 1917 by the H.K. Porter Locomotive Works in Pittsburgh and first used by the U.S. Army at the Watertown Arsenal in Massachusetts. It was purchased by the East Branch & Lincoln Railroad and used by the Parker-Young Company right here in its Lincoln railyard in 1945; it was later sold and used by two local paper companies. It was eventually acquired by Clark's

Section of the East Branch & Lincoln Railroad and locomotive, Loon Mountain, Lincoln. *Author photo.*

Trading Post in Lincoln. However, the first locomotive on display here was the East Branch & Lincoln No. 5, a Baldwin locomotive built in 1906 in Philadelphia, purchased new by the J. Henry Lumber Company in Lincoln and used here until 1969. It was on display at Loon Mountain from 1970 to 1999, until the resort traded it to Clark's Trading Post down the road for the locomotive now on display.

As you turn left out of Loon Mountain, you are now on the final stretch of the Kanc, going through the town of Lincoln. Here are ample places to refuel your vehicle, eat and shop, as well as lodging. Two miles down the road on your left, opposite the junction with I-93, is the White Mountains Visitor Center.

WHITE MOUNTAINS VISITOR CENTER

What to Know

This large and well-run visitor center is located on the very west end of the Kancamagus Highway, right off Interstate 93. It is an excellent place to stop, whether as an end to your journey, or as a starting point if you are traveling the Kanc from Lincoln to Conway. It is a privately owned facility, operated by the White Mountains Attractions Association, a marketing firm for many local attractions, including the Loon Mountain Resort and Clark's Bears. There are excellent restrooms here and a small gift shop, and many guides, brochures and maps are available. This site is also manned by Forest Service rangers, primarily on the weekends during the winter months and usually daily during peak periods, but this is subject to change. The phone number for this visitor center is 603 745 8720, or they can be visited online at https://www. visitwhitemountains.com/plan-your-visit/information-services-and-visitor-centers/whitc-mountains-visitor-center/.

It should be noted that State Route 112, which is the official designation of the Kancamagus Highway, continues on from here for twenty miles until it reaches its end when it joins with U.S. Route 302 in Bath. However, while the views on that part of the highway are also scenic, only that part that runs from Lincoln to Conway is designated as the Kancamagus Highway.

Chapter 7

TREES AND WILDLIFE
ALONG THE KANC

For many, the one main attraction of driving the Kancamagus Highway is the fall foliage viewing opportunities that present themselves every year. And with good reason, for the vast colorful panorama of trees that can be seen here in the White Mountain National Forest every year is one of the most beautiful in the entire country. The varieties of trees found here and the ecology of this mountain hardwood forest are most interesting, yet they are often taken for granted. There is, in fact, more to the forest here than meets the eye. In tandem with the forest, there are also ample opportunities to see the local wildlife in an up-close-and-personal manner while traveling the Kanc. Because much of the area around the highway has remained undeveloped, it has long been considered one of the top places in the state for such viewing activity. With varying amounts of effort, you can see such mammals as the moose, black bear or fox and a wide variety of birds, from the pileated woodpecker to the golden-crowned kinglet, and you can fish for the brown, brook or rainbow trout. These are just a few examples of the abundant wildlife that can be seen in this area of the White Mountain National Forest. Indeed, whether it's at one of the scenic overlooks or one of the several mountain ponds or somewhere along a hiking trail, with a little planning and luck, your trek along the Kanc may combine both forest and wildlife experiences that will remain a fond memory for years to come.

Trees and the Forest

There are a number of tree species to be found in this area of the White Mountain National Forest. The red spruce tree is a medium-sized evergreen that can grow up to 70 feet high and provides a constant green backdrop. The eastern hemlock and the American beech tree are also found in great numbers. The hemlock is an evergreen that does well in the shade. It is long-lived (some hemlocks have been known to live one thousand years) and can grow, albeit slowly, to a height of around 150 feet. It can also be distinguished from other evergreens in that, unlike most trees in its family, the top of the tree is not pointed; rather, it is bushy in appearance. The American beech tree, on the other hand, is a deciduous tree. It can grow to just over 100 feet tall and does well in the shade, a nice survival feature in this forest of big evergreens. It is an important tree in that the nut it produces is a vital food staple for local wildlife (to be discussed shortly). The red maple, the yellow birch and the balsam fir also have a wide distribution. However, there are other trees that can also be found, some of which give much pleasure to tourists and visitors alike, the most popular being the sugar maple (also known as the hard maple) and the white, or paper, birch tree—but you can also see the mountain ash, the northern red oak and the black spruce, as well as the sumac, the basswood, the tupelo, the alder and the pin cherry. Finally, among the softwood trees, we cannot forget the ever-present white pine, which has been commercially important in New Hampshire since colonial times.

One other interesting aspect of this forest that often goes unnoticed is its various zones. Often when one thinks of mountain zones, it might be in relation to larger mountain ranges like those out west in the Rockies or Alaska. But even here in northern New Hampshire, the mountains and their forests have varied zones. At the lowest level, about three thousand feet or lower, the hardwoods are commonly found mixed with evergreens. The soil is good and well drained, and the temperature is suitable for a variety of species. However, in the boreal zone, ranging from three thousand to four thousand feet, there is a marked change. The spruce and fir trees dominate now, though, surprisingly to many, the paper birch also does well at the middle to lower elevations in this zone. While many may think of this tree, popular with tourists for its brilliant white bark, as a weak or vulnerable species, they would be wrong. True, it is not a long-lived tree in general, but it can grow in a wide variety of areas, and it is often the first to return to an area of the forest that has been decimated by a massive blowdown or flooding or damaged from a fire or human activity. The bark of the paper birch is not just a pretty sight; it is also an extraordinary adaptive feature. The white bark actually reflects sunlight and allows the tree to better maintain its interior cell temperature during the wintertime rather than experience the wide fluctuation in temperature from extreme heat to freezing cold that a dark-colored bark might cause. Just as arctic animals like the polar bear and the snowshoe rabbit have white fur to survive in their climate, so, too, does the white birch have a similar adaptation. Additionally, the white birch has an important cultural history, being a prime resource for Native American peoples here for thousands of years. They utilized its bark to cover their dwellings and make birch bark canoes, birch bowls, birch bark baskets and other containers for food preparation and storage.

Finally, getting back to the forest zones here, at the highest elevation, above 4,000 feet, the tree species are by now well thinned out. Black spruce and fir trees are found up to 4,400 feet, but they are stunted in growth and often misshapen. These trees are easily visible with binoculars at the outlooks along the Kanc, and their silhouettes can often be seen on a clear day, their appearance both entrancing and foreboding. Many people believe there is not enough water at this elevation for trees to grow, but this is not the case. The higher elevations have constant cloud cover, so precipitation is seldom the problem. Instead, it is the rocky and thin nature of the soil, making it hard for trees to gain a foothold, as well as a lack of nutrients in the thin soil (vastly different from the rich forest floor soil), that is problematic. Combine this with the extreme wind and weather conditions that are a constant in the White Mountains, and it's no wonder that many of the trees at higher elevations have a stunted or blasted appearance. Once you get above 4,400 feet, there are no trees, and instead, hikers will see the fragile plant ground cover that is nearly identical to that found in the arctic.

So, as you are looking out at the fall foliage panorama at any given spot along the highway, just what kind of leaves are you seeing? Well, those that please the most, perhaps, are those of the sugar maple, which turn bright orange, red or yellow. The sugar maple tree also wins an additional award, as it is the best source for maple syrup, of which much is produced locally in New Hampshire. If you have a fondness for this sweet delicacy, you'll want to pick up a bottle or two of that before you head home—and maybe some maple sugar candy to go along with it. The paper birch is also a strong contributor to fall's colorful palette, its leaves turning a golden yellow, fiery red or bright orange. Other leaves that help to fill in the color schemes viewed here include those of the predominant red maple (deep red or yellow), the northern red oak (a rich red or brown), the mountain ash (mostly red) and the American beech (bronze or copper to yellow), to name just a few. Many visitors are inspired to pick up a few examples of these colorful leaves as souvenirs to bring home with them. No matter how you preserve your memories, when you combine all of these leaf and tree elements together, the results are truly spectacular, and it's no wonder that thousands ride the Kanc annually to take in the scenery.

For fall viewing on the Kanc, the primary season starts in late September, when the weather begins to turn cooler and the leaves begin to change. Leaf peepers (yes, that's what we call fall foliage tourists up here!) need to plan out their trip for maximum effect. If you visit here in early September, while you may see a few (by our standards) colorful trees, you will not experience the forest to the fullest. Peak season usually comes around mid-October, Columbus Day, but can occur on either side of that time by a few days or even more. The vibrance of colors is affected by many factors, including how much rain we've received in the preceding months, possible drought conditions and the transition from warm and sunny days to cooler nights. Ultimately, no two fall seasons are the same. You can check out the State of New Hampshire's tourism website for up-to-date fall foliage conditions anytime in season at https://www.visitnh.gov/seasonal-trips/fall/foliage-reports. Please know that during the Columbus Day holiday weekend in October, the Kancamagus Highway experiences its heaviest traffic and most crowded conditions of the entire year. If you visit at this time, you will still be able to have a wonderful experience but among greater crowds. One alternative is to plan a midweek visit; there will still be other visitors but much fewer in number. It's hard to plan for New Hampshire and White Mountain weather at this time of the year. Sunny conditions will show the leaves to their fullest effect, but don't put off your trip just because it's raining. The views of low clouds hanging over the mountaintops, with perhaps a bit of sun shining through—or the prospect of a rainbow—are still spectacular. Whatever the conditions, be sure to bring a sweatshirt or jacket, as temperatures (and wind) at the higher elevations can make for cool and crisp weather.

MOOSE

This majestic animal is the largest and heaviest of the deer family in North America. It is also one of the primary attractions for those who come to visit New Hampshire and experience the Kancamagus Highway. Indeed, to get a picture of this sometimes-elusive creature is the goal of almost everyone who visits here (and many locals, too). It's not hard to understand why; the animal is bigger than a man and larger examples can weigh in at nearly two thousand pounds. Its distinctive profile includes a large proboscis; its nostrils can be sealed shut when grazing on aquatic vegetation, a nice evolutionary adaptation. The moose is an herbivore whose diet consists of not just water plants but also tree shoots and other non-grass vegetation. An average-sized moose will eat over seventy pounds of food a day. Interestingly, though aquatic plants have a lower caloric value, they provide the salt that moose need in their diet. Moose are the only deer species that can feed underwater, and surprisingly, they have been known to dive down to depths reaching eighteen feet to get their food. The mountain ponds located along the Kancamagus Highway are vital resources for local moose. On land, moose are attracted to saplings and are known to bend these down to their level to feed; their prehensile lip is another adaptation that helps them in the never-ending search for food. If their food is located higher up, moose can even stand on their hind legs to reach as high as fourteen feet. Of course, the most distinctive aspect of their appearance is the antlers of the bull moose, the male of the species. Their racks can have a spread of over seventy inches, though the average for those harvested in New Hampshire is about forty-eight inches. The size and growth of antlers overall is determined by a moose's age and diet, and symmetrical antlers are a sign of its overall health. These antlers are important in the mating process, as females (cows) pick their mates based on the size of their antlers, while bull moose use them both as a display of dominance over other males and to fight their rivals. The moose is a solitary creature by nature, and they do not form herds, though individuals will sometimes feed in proximity to each other. Calves will remain with their mothers for about eight months before being sent off on their own. During the rutting and mating season in September and October, moose are very active, and their calls can be heard far and wide at times. You'll know it when you hear it—it's very loud and distinctive. Since they are often on the move during this time, seeking a mate, they are frequently sighted along the Kanc. Even outside this time, moose are on the move during the day; they are most active near sunrise and near sunset, and they sleep at night. They are often drawn to the Kancamagus Highway during the winter for the salt on the road.

Moose were once prevalent in early New Hampshire, but they were nearly hunted to extinction, there being only some 50 animals left in the state by

Moose crossing area on the eastern end of the Kancamagus Highway. *Author photo.*

the 1950s. However, with a management plan in place, that population has rebounded and now stands at somewhere around 3,300 animals. A moose hunt was revived in the state in 1988 but is strictly controlled by a lottery system, and for 2022 a maximum of 40 animals can be harvested, down over 20 percent from the previous year. This is a good thing, because the moose population has been hit by a growing prevalence of tick-borne diseases, which are currently one of its greatest threats—along with overall climate change—to survival.

Viewing the moose along the Kancamagus Highway can be a varied experience. Those who live in the area and travel it frequently report numerous sightings, while others have never seen one. Generally speaking, the best time for viewing is during the late day/early evening hours or near sunrise. However, at any time of the year, especially during the fall mating season, don't be surprised if you see one in broad daylight. Excellent places to encounter a moose include Lily Pond, Church Pond and Falls Pond. Pemigewasset Overlook and C.L. Graham Wangan Overlook are also excellent possibilities at the right time of the day. Many people drive the Kanc at night during peak times in hopes of seeing a moose. If you don't want to do the driving yourself, consider the experience of a guided moose tour by bus. There are outfits in both Lincoln and Conway that offer moose-sighting tours by bus from May to September. These tours take place in the evening and usually last for several hours. Though they cannot guarantee that you will see a moose, they do advertise a high success rate on their trips. Be sure to book these tours well in advance, as they do fill up rapidly.

BIRDING

Whether you're a casual bird watcher or an avid birder, the Kanc is a great place to seek out our avian friends, which are easily the most viewable of all the wildlife in the White Mountains. The birds that call the area home can be experienced in several different ways. First, they can often be spotted at overlooks and other popular stopping-off points along the highway. These are areas that require little effort or exertion, and whether you're sitting at a picnic table among the pines while at Rocky Gorge or looking out over Lily Pond, with patience and time you will spot the local birds. For those who are willing to venture just a bit farther away but want nothing to do with a full-on hiking expedition, the easy walking trails at Falls Pond, the Forest Discovery Trail, the Albany Town Forest and the trail up to Sabbaday Falls will also result in some nice bird encounters. Finally, for those willing to hike farther afield, these expeditions can result in even greater rewards. Some of these hikes—like those to Church Pond, Sawyer Pond, Mount Potash and Greely and East Ponds—are shorter in distance but can yield excellent sightings of birds that you may not see close to the highway. Go farther afield, perhaps taking a hike that results in summiting such peaks as Mount Osceola, the Tripyramids or Mount Chocorua, and you will see different kinds of birds at these higher altitudes.

So, what kinds of birds are to be seen in this area along the Kanc? Well, this part of the White Mountains is largely songbird country, but woodpeckers, owls, waterfowl and even the occasional raptor can also be spotted. Right off, those familiar members of the corvid family, blue jays, crows and ravens, can easily be spotted at almost every stopping point along the way. In fact, the blue jays are so numerous, especially at the eastern end of the Kanc, that it's not uncommon to see them swooping down in pairs alongside the highway or even crossing in front of your car. Stop a bit at some of these sites, especially in picnic areas in the pines or around the ponds, and many smaller birds will make their presence known, including the black-capped chickadee, the tufted titmouse, blue-headed and red-eyed vireos, the dark-eyed junco, the cedar waxwing, the red-breasted and white-breasted nuthatches, the hermit and Swainson's thrushes, the brown creeper, the American goldfinch, the purple finch (New Hampshire's state bird), the eastern wood pewee, the least flycatcher, the white-throated sparrow, the pine siskin, the eastern phoebe, the robin and the northern cardinal. Also predominating here are several varieties of kinglets, including the ruby and the golden-crowned, as well as their cousins, at least twelve varieties of warblers, including the yellow-rumped warbler, the pine warbler, the Blackburnian warbler, the black-throated green warbler, the black poll warbler, the palm warbler, the Nashville warbler, the black-and-white warbler, the ovenbird, the magnolia warbler, the Cape May warbler and Wilson's warbler. Of these birds, the black-and-white warbler is just one of many favorites. It is known for its distinctive zebra-like black-and-white stripes and is unique among warblers as it spends its time foraging for food on tree trunks, creeping downward as it probes for insects in the bark and moss. It also nests on the forest ground at the base of tree trunks. One of the earliest migrants to arrive in the spring, the black-and-white warbler is not a shy bird and can be easily spotted in the right setting.

While none of the songbirds found in the area around the Kanc are rare and, depending on where you're from, can perhaps easily be found in your backyard feeder at home, what makes birding here so special is the sheer number of species that can be found, as well as the opportunity to easily observe large flocks, many with mixed species. What early birder Frank Bolles noted some 130 years is still true today, that in these flocks "perhaps not more than one in ten will be a chickadee, yet it is the chickadee which gives character and direction to the body....Sometimes a single flock contains nearly all of these couriers of the woods, while

The black-and-white warbler is one of the many species of birds found along the Kancamagus Highway. *Frode Jacobsen, Shutterstock.*

A Canadian jay in the White Mountains. *Drewthehobbit, Shutterstock.com.*

others are composed of a single species." Interestingly, while many of these species predominate in the forest at lower altitudes, a number can also be found in higher zones. The diminutive kinglets are found in every level of the forest and thus are an easy addition to many a birder's life list, while the Canadian jay, also known as the gray jay, is generally only found at higher levels. This bird is popular with hikers. It is distinguished by its distinctive gray, white and black coloring, and its head coloring gives it a hooded appearance. This jay, bold like its blue cousin, is constantly on the lookout for food and is not shy around humans, well known for swooping down and taking food from the palms of hikers or any bit of trail mix that may have been accidentally dropped on the ground.

As to other species, woodpeckers, too, are common, with the downy, hairy and pileated woodpeckers easily found at many locations, as well as the northern flicker, from low-altitude ponds to trails high up on Mount Passaconaway and Mount Whiteface. Owls are also common in the White Mountains but are very difficult to spot for most visitors due to their nocturnal nature. The barred owl lives here year-round and may be spotted if you're lucky, while the same is true for the small (only eight inches long) northern saw-whet owl. The former has been sighted at the Covered Bridge campground, while the latter has been found around Greely Pond. Waterfowl, not surprisingly, are easily found at several of the White Mountain ponds along the Kanc. The easiest viewing is to be had at Lily Pond, where the mallard, the American black duck and the wood duck—the male of the species known for its colorful, crested head—can be spotted. Canada geese are also frequent visitors, especially during migration time. Unfortunately, New Hampshire's most celebrated waterfowl, the common loon, is not commonly found on most of the ponds along the highway. Most are too small for their liking, as loons need a large runway for their takeoffs and landings. The one exception may be Sawyer Pond, which has had a history of loon sightings in the past. While this part of the White Mountains is not noted for its extensive raptor sightings, the turkey vulture is fairly common, while sightings of the bald eagle, northern goshawk, red-tailed hawk, sparrow hawk (the tiniest of the falcons in North America) and peregrine falcons are made from time to time—peregrine falcons had nesting sites at Square Ledge on Mount Passaconaway at least as late as 2020. Finally, there are two mainly terrestrial birds that can be found here that are quite friendly to humans: the ruffled grouse and the wild turkey. The grouse is a chicken-like bird that is about eighteen inches long and is commonly found deep in the woods, likely to be flushed near a hiking trail. The wild turkey is the largest game bird in the state; once hunted to extinction, wild turkeys were reintroduced to the state beginning in the 1960s and are now found everywhere. In the late winter/early spring and in the fall, they are a common sight along the highway, sometimes singly, but often in flocks of as many as ten to twenty birds. They are known for crossing the road with little regard to oncoming traffic but can fly up and over cars. Despite their commonality, I never grow tired of seeing these birds, with their funny and fearless personalities.

In short, there is no shortage of avian species to be seen while visiting the Kanc. While some species call this forest home year-round, the optimal time for a birder's visit is in June, when most migrants have returned and set up housekeeping, while July also is a good month. As is true in many locales, early mornings are when bird populations are the most active along the Kanc, though at higher elevations this time is often extended to the late morning hours. For the most current information as to which species may be seen and where, the eBird website, https://ebirdhotspots.com/birding-in-new-hampshire/, is an excellent resource to check out in advance.

Black Bear

The black bear is the other large mammal that is ubiquitous in the White Mountains, but coming in contact with them is almost always incidental for most visitors. This may come about while a bear is sniffing out a campground or deep in the woods along a hiking trail. Every once in a while, they can be seen ambling across the highway. These clever critters vary in size; males on average weigh anywhere from 125 to 550 pounds, depending on their age, the time of year and their overall health, while females will range in weight from 90 to 375 pounds. Their fur is very soft, with a dense undercoat. Their paws are large for their size, and their claws are thick at the base and taper to a point, being almost identical in length on both the hind and front paws. Black bears are extremely strong and can easily lift objects twice their own weight and more, and they are very dexterous. This, combined with their intelligence, allows them to open door latches and dumpster lids and screw the lids off jars. Their sight is good, and their sense of smell is keen; they are able to pick up scents from over a mile away, whether it be that of a discarded hot dog or a toothpaste tube left uncapped. Black bears can also run fast for short distances. Black bears are usually found within the forest and will seldom venture out into wide-open spaces, though it does happen at times. In the winter, black bears are absent from the landscape, as they go into hibernation in October or November, entering dens that they have hollowed out in tree cavities, under old logs or rocks or in shallow depressions and caves. It's not surprising that geographical features in the area of the Kanc, like Bear Mountain and Bear Notch Road, are named after this animal. It predominates in the White Mountain region and relies heavily on the nuts (or "mast") that come from the American beech trees in the area. These nuts are vitally important to wildlife in the area; the American beech is the only tree here that offers a nutrient-dense food source. Beech nuts are especially important to bears in the fall season, as they consume them in great quantities in preparation for their winter hibernation. Interestingly, when black bears come out of hibernation in the spring, it takes their metabolism some time to return to normal, and they spend the time foraging in their territory come late March and April.

Black bears are omnivores, but the larger part of their diet consists of vegetation, including grasses, nuts, berries and shoots. Their animal diet consists mostly of insects (they love honey) and fish, but in the springtime they will attack fawns if the opportunity arises. Except when they find an opportunity for food, bears do not seek contact with humans. While it is true that food-related encounters with black bears in the White Mountains have been on the rise, it is more likely that during your visit, should you happen to spot one, it will be at a safe distance.

Small Mammals

There are a number of animals, smaller than a moose or a bear, that you may encounter while traveling along the Kancamagus Highway. Some will be easier to spot, like the ubiquitous squirrel; others you might never see, such as the small rodents that many other species feed on. The animals on the list that follows are representative of some of the larger mammals that may be encountered.

The white-tailed deer population in New Hampshire is a large one, though their numbers are not as dense in this part of the White Mountain National Forest as they are farther south or closer to the Connecticut River. Still, the possibility of seeing one of these common but beautiful animals is strong. Bucks, the male of the species, can weigh anywhere from 150 to 300 pounds when fully grown, while does weigh between 90 and 200 pounds. These deer are reddish-brown in the summer, their coats changing to a grayish brown in the winter. They get their name from the white underside of their tail, which they show to members of their group when danger is near. Deer eat plants of all types, including water plants, woody vegetation and nuts. They travel in groups; the family grouping consists of a doe, her young and several bucks, while other groups consist solely of bucks, usually three to five in number. In the winter, various groups will join together, sometimes in large numbers, to provide protection from predators. Deer can run fast, over thirty-five miles per hour, for short distances, and they can jump over eight feet high. They are also excellent swimmers; their hair is specially designed to keep them buoyant. Drivers who are on the Kanc either near dusk or at dawn should be on the lookout, especially during the fall breeding season.

Coyotes may also be seen in the White Mountains, though visitors and locals alike sometimes mistake them for wolves. Wolves were once common in the state but were early on hunted to extinction, many local towns offering a bounty for their hides. While there are wolves in eastern Canada, there is now no credible evidence that wolves have reestablished themselves here. However, the eastern coyote is prevalent throughout New Hampshire.

This was not always the case. The animal was not verified in the state until 1944, but now coyotes are everywhere. The coyote weighs between thirty and fifty pounds, the size of a medium-sized dog, and range in length from five to six feet. Their fur, which is very thick, ranges from a silvery gray to a brownish-red color. They are distinguished by long, thin legs, a pointed snout and a bushy, black-tipped tail that, when they are running, is pointed downward. The coyote takes advantage of whatever food can be found, be it small mammals like mice or squirrels, insects, fruit or even garbage if the opportunity presents itself. Coyotes generally have one mate for life and establish a territory that can range in size between five and twenty-five miles. Their young, as many as eight in a litter, are born in May and, when older, may share the territory with their parents or go off to establish their own territory. Should you happen to hear the well-known long howl of the coyote, know that is their call to bring the members of the pack together, while barking indicates that danger is nearby. Should you have a close encounter with a coyote, whether on a hiking trail or around a campground, exercise normal caution but with the knowledge that these fierce-looking canines really pose no threat to humans.

The red fox is the most common land carnivore found not only in New Hampshire but in all of the United States and Canada. These foxes are distinguished by their rusty-red color, and they have a white underbelly, chin and throat. The backs of their ears and lower legs are black. Despite their name, they have several variations, some rare examples being entirely black; more common are those that are black-haired with silver tips (the silver fox), or reddish-brown with a dark cross on their shoulders. They stand just over two feet tall and average about three feet long. Males usually live a solitary existence for part of the year, except during mating season (January to March). Females will have a litter of up to ten pups, and the family will stay together for about seven months until the kits go off on their own. While the female stays close to the family den, the male will travel many miles to hunt, sometimes well over one hundred. They usually hunt at night, their diet consisting of small mammals and birds but also insects, berries, grasses and acorns. Red foxes are fast, reaching speeds of over forty miles per hour, and can be quite vocal. Their high-pitched screams are often heard at night. In the winter, red foxes grow a dense coat and usually sleep out in the open, curled up and wrapping their bushy tail around their nose and footpads. Though they are nocturnal, it is not uncommon to see a solitary male off in the woods or even crossing the highway in the early morning hours.

The porcupine is a rodent that is often both misnamed and misunderstood. Traditionally, in New Hampshire, they have been termed "hedgehogs," a custom going back to the first colonial settlers who encountered them. While they somewhat resemble the European hedgehog, they are actually an entirely different animal altogether. Mount Hedgehog near the Kancamagus Highway is really misnamed in this regard. The porcupine is very common in the White Mountains and all of the state. They average about two to three feet long, not including their long tail, and weigh somewhere between twelve and thirty-five pounds. They are brown or gray in color and are distinguished by the numerous quills—up to thirty thousand—that cover their coat and serve as defense weapons. Contrary to popular belief, they cannot shoot their quills long-distance, but should you get too close, they can use their tail to whack their enemies. Once embedded under the skin, these quills, which have barbed ends, are hard to remove, as many a New Hampshire dog (and one human I know) has discovered. They mostly eat leaves, twigs and bark, the hemlock tree being a favorite, and are largely nocturnal, living in dens under old tree stumps or rocks. However, the porcupine is an agile climber, and it's not uncommon to see them in a tree during the day; despite their ungainly shape, they are quite a sight to behold in this setting.

Finally, there is that hardworking and busy rodent of the White Mountain streams and ponds, the beaver. This mammal, which can weigh anywhere from thirty to one hundred pounds, is known for its broad, flat, leathery tail, large hind legs and webbed feet. Beavers also have sharp teeth that grow continuously, their incisors constantly worn down by incessant gnawing. They are strictly herbivores, eating aquatic plants, tree bark and twigs among many other kinds of plants. They have small ears but incredible hearing, and they have the ability to close their ears and nose while underwater. The beaver, the largest rodent in North America, is very territorial, their colony area marked by scent mounds and occupying on average about a half a mile of a given waterway. They mate for life and have a litter annually of between three and five kits after reaching maturity. Beavers feed at night but can sometimes be spied by hikers in the morning hours. However, they make their presence well known to all, even if you never see one. They build dams on slow-moving streams and rivers next to woodlands and, once done, construct their lodges usually in the deepest part of the resulting beaver pond or, if the pond is too big, along the bank. They occupy this area until the food supply runs out and then move on to another area to begin their dam-building process all over again. Gnawed tree stumps along a stream, or sometimes a flooded trail, are sure signs of their incredible activity.

Reptiles and Amphibians

There are snakes in the White Mountains and the area around the Kancamagus. However, there are no venomous snakes to be found in New Hampshire, so even if you're not a fan of this type of animal, you have nothing to fear. The timber rattlesnake was once common all over the state but is now an endangered species. There is only one known population, so it's unlikely you'll ever see one, but if you do, you have no need to worry. They use their venom on their prey, mostly small rodents, and are not seeking out human contact. Most likely, if you do encounter a snake, whether around the ponds or on a hiking trail, it will be one of several common snakes that are harmless. The common garter snake is easily found, averaging about twenty inches long and distinguished by the several stripes—yellow, brown or green—that run vertically down its body. The ringneck snake is also common in the area, being about a foot long and bluish black in color, with a golden ring around its neck and a yellow underbelly. Finally, the northern red-bellied snake might also be spied, but these snakes are small, only eight to ten inches long, brown or gray in color with—you guessed it—a red underbelly.

Turtles are increasingly a dwindling animal in New Hampshire, but it is the eastern painted turtle that is the most common species and likely to be found in this area. They are about four to six inches long, known for the yellow spot behind each eye and the red and yellow stripes on the head and neck. As to frogs, the brownish-green bullfrog is common in pond areas, while small wood frogs can be found in wooded areas as well as along small streams and in ponds and bogs. Other species of frogs and toads that can be found here are the pickerel frog; the northern leopard frog (which is a species of special concern); the ever-present American toad; the commonly heard spring peeper, whose songs serenade visitors in the evening hours; and the hard-to-spot gray tree frog.

Finally, salamanders, though hard to spot, also make this area home. Among those species present are the blue-spotted salamander (which spends most of its time underground), the tiny northern dusky salamander, the large spotted salamander, the small northern redback salamander and the small northern two-lined salamander.

Fishing

The Swift River and the ponds along the Kancamagus Highway offer many opportunities for both the novice and expert angler. The Swift River is known for its sports fishing and has an interesting natural history. It was once home to the Atlantic salmon, which hatched here and had a free passage down to the Atlantic Ocean as adults, subsequently returning upriver to spawn in the Swift River annually. However, the salmon would eventually disappear from the Swift River as development took place and dams were built farther downriver in Maine, which prevented the salmon from making their return. Today, the Swift River has to be periodically restocked by the state with rainbow, brown and brook trout (raised in hatcheries) because the take of sports fishermen annually exceeds the reproductive capacity of the fish themselves. On the upper Swift River, the "High Country native brook trout...are considered the jewels of the North Country and prized by many," according to expert angler Randy Ouellette; they range up to fourteen inches in length. Some sections of the river are easily accessible and thus popular spots, especially around the Albany Covered Bridge. Those who want a less crowded fly-fishing experience, and hopefully more fish, will have to hike or wade to some of the more remote spots on the river. Many will even hire a local guide to take them to sites where the fish will bite. There are currently no restrictions as to where fly-fishing can be conducted on the Swift River.

The ponds and streams along the Kanc are also stocked with trout; some of those in remote locations, like Sawyer and Greely Ponds, are aerially stocked by helicopter on a yearly basis. Though the brook trout predominates and is the most popular among anglers, other fish may also be caught in these ponds. These include the pickerel and the hornpout. The latter, as anglers well know, is a type of catfish that is commonly found all over the state. It was once New Hampshire's most popular fish but no longer. They can live in warm, low-oxygen waters, are bottom-feeders and only grow to about eight inches long. While they can be a tough fish to catch and, once caught, difficult to handle because of their barbels, they are considered to be excellent eating.

Chapter 8

CAMPING ALONG THE KANC

For those who'd like to enjoy what the area has to offer during an extended stay, there are many opportunities for camping along the Kancamagus Highway. This section details the six available campgrounds, and one cabin, owned by the Forest Service. It does not include any private campgrounds located outside the area that may be in proximity. There are also opportunities for backcountry hiking, the guidelines for which are discussed in the following pages. If this is your first trip to New Hampshire or the White Mountains and the Kancamagus Highway, with a little planning, your experience will be a memorable one.

It is advised that campers visiting the White Mountain National Forest plan accordingly and arrive early, especially during peak weekend times, and it is always best to have a backup plan if the campground of your choice should happen to be full. However, if you're camping anytime from Sunday through Friday, you should have no problem finding a spot during peak times. The campsites in the White Mountain National Forest are well planned out. For the most part, they are large in size, level and, where conditions warrant, elevated so as to be dry. Though most of these campgrounds provide the bare necessities in terms of facilities, they are priced accordingly, and the rates are quite affordable.

The camping or cabin sites that follow are listed in order as you travel from Conway to Lincoln.

Covered Bridge Campground

Located on the Passaconaway/Dugway Road, six miles west of Conway on the north side of the Swift River, this site is one of the largest Kancamagus campgrounds. Please be aware that access from the Kancamagus Highway is limited, and if your vehicle is over seven feet, nine inches in height, you will not be able to make it across the bridge to reach the campground. Instead, you will have to access it by taking Passaconaway Road from Conway. This campground has forty-nine sites in all, about half of which may be reserved; check the online map for details. Water is available at two spots, and vault toilets are available at seven locations. There are no shower facilities. This campground is a popular one due to its proximity to the covered bridge and the Swift River, offering opportunities for fishing off a pier and wading into the river. Early morning or sunset and evening walks through the Albany Covered Bridge offer a pleasant experience and scenic views. Also close at hand is the Boulder Loop hiking trail, which rewards one with fine views of the surrounding mountains.

Blackberry Crossing Campground

This campground is located six miles west of Conway, right off the Kancamagus Highway and directly across the highway from the Albany Covered Bridge. It offers twenty-six campsites, all of which are filled on a first-come, first-served basis, with no reservations accepted. Six of the sites are walk-in tent sites only, and there are three vault toilets sites available here but no shower facilities. There is one centrally located water pump. This campground is also the historic site of a CCC camp that once existed here from 1935 to 1942 (discussed in chapter 6). Its proximity to the covered bridge, as well as the popular Lower Falls Scenic Area, makes this campground a Kancamagus favorite.

Jigger Johnson Campground

Named after a famed White Mountains lumberjack and trapper, this campground is the largest of all those located on the Kancamagus, being 12.5 miles west of Conway, and one of the most popular. It has seventy-five sites, many of them close to the Swift River, which are served by five flush-

Campground on Dugway Road, White Mountain National Forest, 1932. *National Archives, courtesy Forest History Society.*

View of Blackberry Campground, 1962. Note the Rambler station wagon (*left*) and possibly a Robin Hood camp trailer (*right*). *National Archives, courtesy Forest History Society.*

toilet facilities and coin-operated showers (the only ones located on the Kanc). There are eleven spots where water can be obtained. This campground is also located adjacent to the Russell-Colbath House Historic Site; the two are connected by a small path. In the summer, programs are sometimes held in the modern barn at the historic site for the enjoyment of campers. All of the campsites here are filled on a first-come, first-served basis.

RADEKE CABIN

This site is the only one of its kind to be found along the Kancamagus Highway. It is fourteen miles west of Conway, located on the right side of the highway. The Radeke Cabin used to be owned by the University of New Hampshire (UNH) and served as a summer camp for the school's forestry students until it was acquired by the Forest Service in 1969. It is extremely rustic in nature, and visitors (up to ten allowed) should be prepared to bring everything they will need. The nightly rates for this cabin, while overall reasonable, are about three times higher than that of the regular campground sites listed here. The cabin has a woodstove, for which the wood is supplied during the wintertime only (in the summer visitors must bring their own), but there is no electricity, water or indoor plumbing. There is a pit toilet located outdoors just a short distance away. The house does have a wheelchair ramp for accessibility. Inside, the cabin is divided into three rooms, with ten bunks in all. Visitors should be aware that there is very little insulation, so it can be quite cold inside, even with the woodstove going; sleeping bags are a must. The cabin is also available to rent during the winter and early spring season. Outdoors, the site has a campfire ring, but visitors must bring their own firewood for outdoor use. Additional rules prohibit outdoor camping within a quarter mile of the cabin (including RVs) and stipulate that prior to the reservation check-in date, guests must call the Saco River Ranger Station (603 447 5448) to verify the lock combination. Radeke Cabin is a carry in, carry out site, so visitors must bring trash bags and should be aware that upon arrival, they may need to clean the cabin, as the Forest Service cannot always do so in between occupants. Upon departure, guests must clean up after themselves and make sure all windows are closed and doors locked. As to features, the cabin is near the Swift River, and just a quarter mile away can be found the Downes Brook, UNH and Mount Potash trails.

Passaconaway Campground

Located fifteen miles west of Conway, this campground is near Sabbaday Falls. There are thirty-three campsites here, some close to the Swift River. No reservations are accepted at this campground, all being filled on a first-come, first-served basis. There are three vault toilet facilities here and four places where water can be obtained. This campground is also the site of the trailhead for the Church Pond Trail (discussed in the next chapter), the Church Ponds being just over a mile away. Across the highway may also be found the trailheads for the Downes Brook Trail, which leads to Mount Whiteface (3,985 ft.); the University of New Hampshire (UNH) Trail, which leads to Mount Hedgehog (2,520 ft.); and the Mount Potash Trail, which leads to the mountain of the same name. All these trails are discussed in the next chapter.

Big Rock Campground

This campground is one of two on the western end of the Kancamagus Highway, located six miles east of Lincoln. It offers twenty-eight campsites, of which seventeen are available for reservations. Three vault toilet facilities are available here, as well as two watering sites. Some sites are for tenting only. Named after the big boulders in the area, this is one of the easier campgrounds in which to find a site.

Hancock Campground

Located close by the East Branch Pemigewasset River, this campground is the only one on the Kancamagus Highway which is open year-round. No reservations of any kind are accepted here. Hancock offers fifty-six sites in all, of which twenty-one are walk-in/tent-only sites closest to the river. The site has three toilet facilities, one with flush toilets near the parking lot for the walk-in sites, and four watering sites. Some sites are equipped with bear boxes so that campers may keep their food secure. This is a popular campground that often fills up quickly on peak weekends. Not only is it close to several hiking trails—including the Lincoln Woods Trail, which starts right across the highway—but the swimming spots in the river here are an added bonus. Though Hancock Campground is open in the winter, not all services, including water, are available, though the parking lot is plowed.

Backcountry Camping

This more primitive type of experience, which involves choosing and setting up your own campsite in the wilderness, is permissible in the White Mountain National Forest. Many backcountry campers park at trailheads along the Kancamagus Highway to make their trip into the woods. It is always best to plan ahead for such a camping trip, as there are additional rules that campers must follow. If parking at a trailhead, a parking pass may be required, and signs at the entrance will give information as to what is permitted in the area. First and foremost, setting up campsites within one-quarter of a mile of the Kancamagus Highway, Bear Notch Road and Dugway/Passaconaway Road is prohibited. It is also prohibited to set up your site within one-quarter mile of any trailhead, as well as Sabbaday Falls, Champney Falls and the East Branch Pemigewasset River. It is recommended that camping groups be limited to no more than ten people in most areas, though if you're backcountry camping within the Pemigewasset Wilderness, this is a strict limit. Fires are allowed, but campers are strongly advised to minimize their impact on the forest, and portable stoves are advised to be used whenever possible. It is also the rule that you must carry out what you carry in and leave nothing behind. Human waste should be buried in a hole that is at least four inches deep. Finally, as with any outdoor activity in the White Mountains, be prepared for whatever the weather may bring and make sure you have all the gear you need. It is here worth stating again that there is no cell phone service along most areas of the Kanc, and it is always best practice to inform close family or friends of your plans and when you are scheduled to return.

Chapter 9

HIKING ALONG THE KANC

The Kancamagus Highway serves as the perfect gateway for hikers and outdoor enthusiasts who wish to enjoy the southern White Mountains up close and personal. In all, there are some seventeen trails for serious hikers leading directly off the Kanc (not including additional trails which intersect with these along the way), some very popular, which lead to mountainous sites all over the area. Some of these are relatively short in distance, while others pose greater challenges. No matter which hiking trails you may choose, all have their rewards when it comes to wilderness scenery. Many of these trails have a historic aspect to them, utilizing old logging roads or old railroad beds that date back over one hundred years. In fact, along some of them, remnants of logging camps may be seen, which just adds to the exploration aspect of the hike.

While I have previously listed a few trails under the attractions section, these are simple and short trails that can be experienced by the most casual of visitors, including children, with no planning, hiking gear or major time commitment required. In this section, most of the hiking trails listed will require some forethought and planning, as well as a greater time commitment, usually two hours or more at the least. Many of the trails listed below, such as Boulder Loop and Lincoln Woods, are well packed and very popular with winter hikers, some intersecting with cross-country skiing trails.

A bird's-eye topographical map view of the White Mountains, 1890. The Kancamagus Highway runs straight through the middle of this landscape. *Library of Congress.*

The information that follows for each of these trails is meant as a general description only and is not intended to be definitive. Hikers should consult a reliable, current guide, of which many are available. The best of these is the AMC's *White Mountain Guide.* As of this writing, it is in its thirtieth edition, and its maps and trail descriptions are considered by most hikers to be the most authoritative available. It has been in print for over one hundred years and is well worth the price. I have used its mileage figures for each trail listed below, though these can vary slightly among various guides and other sources. It should be noted that while a number of these trails also have other, sometimes main, access points, all mileage figures here are based on entering the trail from along the Kancamagus Highway.

The trails off the Kancamagus Highway are listed in order when traveling from east to west from Conway to Lincoln. All are within the White Mountain National Forest.

Boulder Loop Trail

DISTANCE: 3.1-mile loop.

TRAILHEAD LOCATION: Just west of the entrance to the Covered Bridge Campground on Dugway/Passaconaway Road, 6 miles west of Conway.

DESCRIPTION: This hiking loop will take about two hours, and hikers can start at either side of the loop, although the left branch is considered the best. Though it rises over nine hundred feet in elevation, it is considered a relatively easy hike for the experienced hiker. As its name implies, there are many large boulders along the way, but hikers are rewarded with views of the Swift River valley and the Sandwich Range when they take the spur path and continue to the viewing ledges. This is a very family-friendly trail and is a go-to trail for many local hikers; it's "fantastic in all seasons," according to veteran hiker Jonny Lovering, being well maintained in the winter.

Champney Brook Trail

DISTANCE: 3.8 miles round trip to Champney Falls, 7.6 miles round trip to the summit of Mount Chocorua via the Piper Trail.

TRAILHEAD LOCATION: 11.5 miles west of Conway on the south side of the highway.

DESCRIPTION: This is a popular and heavily traveled trail that leads to Champney and Pitchers Falls, which are located side by side and emanate from two brooks that flow from the side of Mount Chocorua and converge here. Despite the distance, the hike to the falls is a fairly easy one for most. Champney Falls is a series of cascading falls that drops seventy feet in all, and it has a nice pool. However, the most impressive feature here is actually Pitcher Falls, which can be seen in a gorge to the left. Though accessible, it is harder to reach, being about one hundred feet off the trail. This waterfall has a thirty-five-foot drop into a flume, which can be spectacular, if your visit comes at the right time of the year. The towering walls on both sides of the falls are awe-inspiring. If you're visiting in the spring when the melt-off is still occurring, the waterflow at both sites will be impressive, but it can be much less so in the summer months. From Champney Falls, the trail runs 3.2 miles to the Piper Trail and thence to the summit of Mount Chocorua.

Bolles Trail

DISTANCE: 11.4 miles round trip to Brook Trail.

TRAILHEAD LOCATION: This trail starts near the Champney Falls Trail, and parking is in the same lot, 11.5 miles west of Conway.

DESCRIPTION: This trail passes between Mount Chocorua and Mount Paugus and meets up with the Brook Trail, which then intersects with Liberty Trail to make the summit of Mount Chocorua. This trail uses old logging roads and even passes through the site of an old logging camp close to its junction with Brook Trail. In this area, the blackberry bushes make the trail more difficult to follow, and it was the same over one hundred years ago, when Frank Bolles wrote of the "strong, quarrelsome blackberry" and the "blackberry jungle." Some things never change, as the trail today follows the route of an earlier trail, dubbed by Bolles the "lost trail," which he helped cut in 1892 from an even older abandoned road. Bolles Trail crosses Paugus Brook or its tributaries four times and Twin Brook eleven times, so it can be wet at times of high water. About half a mile from the junction with Brook Trail, you will see a huge mound on the right, which is the Paugus Mill sawdust pile. It is a testimony to just how much timber—and for how long—was cut and processed in this area.

Oliverian Brook Trail

DISTANCE: 10 miles round trip to summit of Mount Passaconaway, via three other trails.

TRAILHEAD LOCATION: One mile west of Bear Notch Road on the south side of the Kancamagus Highway.

DESCRIPTION: This trail to Mount Paugus follows an old railroad bed, an old spur line of the Swift River Railroad for a short time, then an old logging road for a ways. The grade is fairly easy, and the trail makes several water crossings. There is an interesting beaver pond located a mile from the trailhead that can cause flooding and wet conditions. At mile 1.9, the trail meets up with the Passaconaway Cutoff, which provides the easiest access to the summit of beautiful Mount Passaconaway, via Square Ledge Trail, and Walden Trail. This portion of the hike involves much steeper grades and rough conditions.

SAWYER POND TRAIL

DISTANCE: 9 miles round trip to Sawyer Pond and back.

TRAILHEAD LOCATION: The parking lot for this trail is located off a small side road from the Kancamagus Highway, 1.4 miles west of Bear Notch Road.

DESCRIPTION: Soon after leaving the parking lot and passing through a clearing, the Swift River must be crossed. This can be dangerous during periods of high water, so exercise caution, and plan on getting wet. After entering the woods, the trail forks, so bear to the left, after which a ski trail joins it. At 1.1 miles, another trail, the Brunel Trail, goes to the right. At 1.7 and 2.6 miles, old logging roads are passed. As you are hiking on this trail, you are climbing the slopes of Birch Hill before coming to a low divide, the trail rising in elevation overall some nine hundred feet. The trail shortly runs close to a small stream before bearing left and away, thereafter heading to Sawyer Pond. As you reach the pond, there are many side paths. Stay on the Sawyer Pond Trail, and it will turn left and cross an outlet brook to the pond at 4.5 miles. From here it is but a short hike north, if you so choose, to Little Sawyer Pond. Sawyer Pond is forty-seven acres in size, Little Sawyer eleven acres. At the former, picnicking, camping, fishing and swimming are all suitable activities. The average depth of Sawyer Pond is forty-eight feet, and there are several places that offer nice access for swimmers and many places to enjoy the scenery. The views here of Mount Tremont, which dominates the skyline, are very beautiful, with Owl's Cliff and Greens Cliff also in sight. Sawyer Pond is notable in that it is one of the few in the White Mountains that actually has an island, located in the northeast corner of the pond and resembling a small knoll from a distance. Little Sawyer Pond, according to author Steven D. Smith, is a "hidden gem," its small size and the towering form of Mount Tremont giving it "a lovely, remote feel, quite different from the expanse of Big Sawyer."

UNH Trail

DISTANCE: A 4.8-mile loop to Mount Hedgehog.

TRAILHEAD LOCATION: From the Downes Brook Trail parking lot, 15 miles west of Conway, south side of the highway opposite Passaconaway Campground.

DESCRIPTION: This trail is so named because the University of New Hampshire once had a forestry camp in the area. At times it follows an old railroad bed or an old logging road. The summit of Mount Hedgehog is reached after a trek of 2.9 miles. The ledges here offer nice views in all directions.

Downes Brook Trail

DISTANCE: Round trip of 12.4 miles to the summit of Mount Whiteface via the Kate Sleeper and Rollins Trails.

TRAILHEAD LOCATION: The trailhead is 15 miles west of Conway on the south side of the highway.

DESCRIPTION: This trail crosses Downes Brook ten times and can therefore be difficult or even impassable at some times of the year, depending on rainfall. It follows for a time an old logging road and at the 3-mile mark passes through an old logging camp. Around mile 4 you can start to get views of the slope of Mount Whiteface, and at mile 5.2 the trail meets up with the Kate Sleeper Trail. Turn left on this trail and continue for .8 miles before reaching the Rollins Trail. This trail offers the best views from ledges below the summit of Mount Whiteface, which is reached in .2 miles.

Mount Potash Trail

DISTANCE: Round trip of 3.8 miles to the summit of Mount Potash.

TRAILHEAD LOCATION: Accessed from the Downes Brook Trail parking lot (see preceding page).

DESCRIPTION: As is written in the *White Mountain Guide*, this trail offers "excellent views for relatively little effort." Before the first mile has been traversed, you will pass through a very pleasing hemlock forest, and by mile 1.6 you begin climbing the side of the mountain. Along the way is a series of ledges, one of which provides a nice view of the valley below, before reaching the summit. These are perfect places for basking and enjoying a nice lunch. The views of the Sandwich Range are impressive, as are those north of the Kancamagus Highway.

Church Pond Trail

DISTANCE: Round trip of 2.2 miles.

TRAILHEAD LOCATION: Near campsite no. 19 in the Passaconaway Campground, 15 miles west of Conway. If no parking is available here, park in the Downes Brook Trail lot directly across the highway.

DESCRIPTION: This is a fairly level hike through an area of pine and spruce swamps and bogs and thus offers up a very different view of the ecology of the White Mountain National Forest. Plan on getting wet on this hike, and water shoes are a must, according to veteran hiker Tina Marconi. Almost right away, the Swift River will have to be forded twice in succession, the first crossing being the main channel. This can be difficult at certain times of the year, and if the water is very high, the trail will be impassable. Once you make it across here, another channel of the river will have to be crossed, but it is usually less difficult. The trail can be difficult to follow because of the dense growth, but continue on and at mile .3 you will meet up with the eastern end of the Nanomocomuck Ski Trail. Bear left here and continue through a red spruce forest. Shortly, you will junction with the western part of the ski trail, but continue on. Thereafter, the Church Pond Trail bears

View of Church Pond, with Green's Cliff looming in the distance. *Courtesy John Compton.*

left and crosses an extensive bog, which is very wet and muddy, crossing many log bridges. The trail intersects with another trail. Take the left fork and continue on a short distance before the trail ends on an eminence known simply as "the Knoll," which overlooks Church Pond. The scenery here is beautiful, offering a view northward of Greens Cliff, as well as Owl's Cliff and Mount Tremont to the east, while to the south can be seen the Tripyramids and Mount Potash. There are graveled paths that lead to the shore of the pond, the main one leading to a big flat boulder that offers a nice spot for a picnic or quiet contemplation. Fishing is allowed in Church Pond, but swimming is not recommended.

Sabbaday Brook Trail

Distance: Round trip of 10.8 miles to North Peak Mount Tripyramid via the Pine Bend Brook and Mount Tripyramid Trails.

Trailhead Location: The trailhead is 15.4 miles west of Conway on the south side of the highway.

Description: The first .3 miles of this trail lead to Sabbaday Falls, which I have previously described, and is a fairly easy trek for most hikers. The Sabbaday Brook Trail continues from the top of the falls and at 1.2 miles bears right onto an old logging road. For the next 2 miles, this trail through the Sandwich Wilderness crosses Sabbaday Brook four times and can be very difficult to follow. It then starts an upward climb toward the valley between Mount Tripyramid and the Fool Killer, a subsidiary peak. This 3,548-foot peak gained its unusual name early on, as those viewing it from afar did not realize that this ridge was separated from Mount Tripyramid by a deep valley. The trail continues on, passing the base of an old rockslide and crossing the brook several more times, the last time at 4.1 miles. It subsequently passes an outlook to Mount Passaconaway. The going from here is rough for a time before the trail levels off and joins the Pine Bend Brook Trail. From here, the summit of North Tripyramid can be reached in .5 miles by going to the right, while to the left Middle Tripyramid peak can be reached in .3 miles. The climb to North Tripyramid is quite harsh, being very steep going.

Pine Bend Brook Trail

Distance: 8 miles round trip to North Peak Mount Tripyramid.

Trailhead Location: 1 mile west of Sabbaday Falls on the south side of the highway. There is no parking lot, so park on the shoulder of the road.

Description: This trail into the Sandwich Wilderness has many brook crossings that can be difficult at certain times of the year. In the beginning it follows the old bed of the Swift River Railroad and an old logging road. At about the 2.5-mile mark you can see Mount Carrigain and Mount Lowell, and at the 3.2-mile mark the trail meets up with the Scaur Ridge Trail. Views of the North Slide are to be had here as you continue onward. The approach to Mount Tripyramid is very steep and rough, and many of the rock ledges are slippery. The final ascent to the summit of North Peak is via the Mount Tripyramid Trail, which meets up with Pine Bend Brook Trail less than one hundred feet from the summit near the North Slide. The best views are to be had just a short distance down the very steep Mount Tripyramid Trail, while the summit of North Peak is wooded. Descending down this trail can be "tricky," according to veteran hiker Tina Marconi, and overall, the Tripyramids are some of the least popular among veteran "peak-baggers" in New Hampshire.

SAWYER RIVER TRAIL

DISTANCE: 3.8 miles to Sawyer River Road.

TRAILHEAD LOCATION: It is located 3.1 miles west of the Sabbaday Falls parking area, with parking on the shoulder of the road.

DESCRIPTION: This trail is not one of the more popular hikes in the area, and much of it covers open ground, except for one small wooded area. Because it follows the old bed of the Sawyer River Railroad, its grades are fairly easy. At .3 miles, the trail crosses the Swift River, which can be difficult at certain times of the year. From here, it conjoins the Nanomocomuck Ski Trail for a time, then follows the west bank of Meadow Brook before crossing it at mile 1.3. From here, it passes several swampy areas and continues on, passing an old logging road before coming into a clearing known as Hayshed Field. At the 2.6-mile mark, the trail junctions with the Hancock Notch Trail, which leads to Mount Hancock. The trail subsequently makes several brook crossings and passes near a bog, reachable by a side trail. After crossing the Sawyer River, the trail meets up with the Sawyer Pond Trail before reaching the trail gate and parking lot beyond.

LIVERMORE TRAIL

DISTANCE: Either 7.7 miles one way to Livermore Road parking lot in Waterville Valley or 13.1 miles round trip after making the complete loop over the Tripyramid summits via the Mount Tripyramid Trail from the north and returning from where the south end meets with the Livermore Trail.

TRAILHEAD LOCATION: The trailhead is 19 miles west of Conway across from Lily Pond. Parking is along the shoulder of the south side of the highway.

Description: This trail is an interesting one and is historically important as it once connected the town of Waterville (now Waterville Valley) to the town of Livermore (now a ghost town) via the Sawyer River Railroad. It is important today, as it connects with many other trails in the area. The trail begins from the Kanc on an old logging road and near mile 1.0 passes the site of an old logging camp. At mile 1.7, it crosses a brook at the bottom of a deep gorge, then ascends steeply, reaching Livermore Pass at mile 2.1. Shortly thereafter, the area is muddy and the trail poorly marked, but at mile 2.7 a gravel road is reached at the Flume Brook Camp clearing. The trail crosses Flume Brook at mile 2.9 then descends steadily, turning along the way and reaching the Scaur Ridge Trail at 3.9 miles. At 4.1 miles, it reaches the northern part of the Mount Tripyramid Trail. This is the best way to summit the peaks of the Tripyramids, as ascending the North Slide is easier than descending it when coming from the south due to the steepness of the rocks. Once you have made these summits, the south end of Mount Tripyramid Trail meets up with Livermore Trail again. Here you can turn back north to reach the Kanc. Should you choose not to summit the Tripyramids, the Livermore Trail continues on and at about the 5.4-mile mark passes some pleasant cascades on Avalanche Brook to the left. A number of local trails are subsequently crossed in the next several miles. After making the second of two crossings over the Mad River, you are now close to the Livermore Road parking area.

Hancock Notch Trail

Distance: Round trip of 9.8 miles to both summits of Mount Hancock via the Cedar Brook and Hancock Loop Trails.

Trailhead Location: The parking lot of the Hancock Overlook on the hairpin turn. Parking is not allowed on the roadside here, and vehicles towing trailers are prohibited from entering the overlook parking lot. The trail begins at the west end of the parking lot and crosses the Kancamagus Highway at this dangerous point. Care must be taken by hikers when making this crossing.

Description: This trail is wide and well marked and is a popular one with hikers; one veteran hiker calls it "primeval" and "sweet." It follows an old railroad bed at first and at mile .6 requires a stream crossing. The trail continues on toward the North Fork Hancock Branch but does not cross it, veering right at the 1.5-mile mark. From here it follows an old logging road and junctions with an old railroad grade (do not follow this as it crosses the river). It then descends and crosses three streams in quick succession before reaching the junction with the Cedar Brook Trail at 1.8 miles. Turn left onto this trail, where you will immediately cross a small brook. The trail continues on the old logging road and between the 2.0- and 2.4-mile marks crosses the North Fork three times. At 2.5 miles, the trail joins with the Hancock Loop Trail, less than two hundred yards beyond the final North Fork crossing. Turn right onto the Loop trail, and you will soon recross North Fork, then cross a rocky stream bed, which can be wet at times. The loop junction is reached after a trek of 1.1 miles (3.6 miles overall on all trails). From here, the two summits of Mount Hancock can be reached in either direction. Unfortunately, the view from both summits is not great, making them less popular peaks to summit than others in the White Mountains. The North Link Trail veers left at the loop junction and starts out flat but soon becomes very steep and difficult. The summit is reached at the .7-mile mark and offers limited views of the Sandwich Range and Mount Osceola from a ledge on a short side path. From this summit, continue on the Ridge Link Trail that connects both the north and south summits of Hancock. It descends to several cols before climbing a ridge to make the south summit at mile 1.4. Here, a short path leads to a nice eastern view of the Sawyer River valley.

GREELY PONDS TRAIL

DISTANCE: Round trip of 4.4 miles to lower Greely Pond.

TRAILHEAD LOCATION: The trailhead is 4.5 miles east of Lincoln Woods parking lot.

DESCRIPTION: The trail begins from the small parking lot here. At .3 miles, it reaches two branches of the South Fork Hancock Branch, which have to be forded because there are no bridges. From here the trail ascends, going over many bridges in the boggy terrain. The height of land is reached at 1.3 miles; the trail then passes the Mount Osceola Trail and through the Mad River Notch. The trail reaches upper Greely Pond at mile 1.7. Here, a side path leads to an outlet brook and a small beach that affords some nice views. Continuing on, the southwest corner of lower Greely Pond is reached at the 2.2-mile mark. The shore of this pond can be reached by a small side path. For most of this trail, the grades are easy. Because of its relative ease, this can be a very busy trail early on in the season.

Both ponds are stocked with brook trout, and fishing is allowed, but swimming is only recommended at upper Greely Pond. Camping is not permitted in the Greely Ponds Scenic Area. Upper Greely Pond is two acres in size and has a depth ranging from nineteen to twenty-seven feet. There are fine views along its shore of Mount Kancamagus, the face of East Peak Osceola Mountain and a spur of Mount Huntington. The spruce and fir trees along the pond's shore are, despite their short stature (caused by the harsh environment), old-growth timber, some trees being as old as 150 years. This is also a prime spot to gather several varieties of mushrooms (if you know what to look for). Lower Greely Pond is three acres in size but only three to four feet deep. It is not suitable for swimming because of the many submerged trees and branches, but the views of Mount Kancamagus and Mad River Notch are excellent. The side path leading to the shore on the pond's southwest corner offers an excellent spot to stop for a picnic and enjoy the views before heading back toward the Kanc. Moose can be seen at Greely Ponds and, even if not seen, evidence of their presence is not hard to spot.

East Pond Trail

DISTANCE: Round trip of 14.4 miles via the East Pond Loop and Little East Pond Trails.

TRAILHEAD LOCATION: The trailhead is 3.7 miles east of the Lincoln Woods parking lot at a bridge over the Hancock Branch.

DESCRIPTION: The first part of this trail follows the bed of an old logging railroad spur until it reaches the crossing of Pine Brook at the .8-mile mark. This crossing can be difficult at some times during the year, depending on rainfall. At mile 2.0, Cheney Brook is crossed, and at mile 2.9, the height of land is reached. The trail then descends on an old logging road, heading right on the western shore of East Pond. At the 3.7 mile mark the East Pond

Trail intersects with the East Pond Loop. Turn right and continue on this for 1.5 miles, until the Little East Pond Trail is reached. Here, the trail turns left and follows the Little East Pond Trail for 1.7 miles before rejoining the East Pond Trail. Believe it or not, in the woods off to the left in this area there was once an industrial site. This was the old Tripoli Mill, which was operated by the Livermore Tripoli Company from about 1911 to 1919. Operations here dredged a mineral known as tripoli or "rotten stone" from East Pond. The substance is a finely powdered and porous rock that was used in those days as an abrasive, employed by photographers to clean and polish the metal surface of daguerreotype plates. Even now it is used as a buffing compound for metals and is considered a hazardous and carcinogenic substance. From the mill here, where blackberry bushes now grow, the processed tripoli was transported to market by the Woodstock & Thornton Gore Railroad, a local logging railroad. The Tripoli Road is named after this mill. Continuing on our hike, turn left on the East Pond Trail and follow it to its junction with the East Pond Loop Trail in 1.2 miles. From here, continue on the East Pond Trail back toward the Kancamagus Highway trailhead.

East Pond is 6.5 acres in size and has a depth of sixteen to twenty-seven feet. Both swimming and fishing are allowed here, the pond being stocked with trout. The views of Mount Osceola and Scar Ridge are impressive. Little East Pond is just 3 acres in size and is only several feet deep and is believed to have no fish. This pond is much closer to Scar Ridge, so the view here is impressive, though there are no great points to sit and enjoy the view at length.

Lincoln Woods Trail

DISTANCE: Round trip of 6.8 miles to Franconia Falls via the Franconia Falls Trail.

TRAILHEAD LOCATION: Lincoln Woods parking lot, 5.6 miles east of the White Mountains Visitor Center at the junction of I-93.

DESCRIPTION: This trail is probably the most popular of them all along the Kancamagus Highway. It can be reached from both sides of the East Branch Pemigewasset River, including by crossing the suspension bridge just below the ranger station. The trail turns right after the suspension bridge and follows the old rail bed of the East Branch & Lincoln Railroad. The trail is wide and well graded, and the rise in elevation is very small, this being the reason many guides rate this trip as a pleasant "stroll" rather than a true hike. At mile .7, there is a fine view of Mount Hancock, after which the trail crosses Osseo Brook and follows it for a short distance before the Osseo Trail goes off to the left. At mile 1.7, the clearing of an old logging camp is passed on the left, and the trail passes close to the river. In this area Bondcliff can be seen upriver. The trail then crosses Birch Island Brook and meets up with Black Pond Trail at 2.6 miles. At 2.9 miles, the trail meets up with the Franconia Falls Trail, which diverges to the left. This trail rises very slightly in elevation, as it parallels Franconia Brook closely at first. At .4 miles, side paths lead out to Franconia Falls, while the trail continues for another .1 miles before ending at a high bank that overlooks a gorge and offers a view of North Hancock Mountain. While these waterfalls are neither the largest nor the most spectacular to be found in New Hampshire, they are beautiful and offer excellent swimming opportunities, with slabs of rock and many pools that vary in size and depth. There are also two excellent natural water slides here; the one closest to the main falls is about twenty feet long and leads into a pool about seven feet deep. However, care must be taken here when the water flow is at a moderate or high level and more turbulent, and accidents have happened here that have resulted in loss of life over the years. Veteran hiker Tina Marconi calls this trail "easy, flat, and glorious…quite beautiful." She also mentions that this trail is "sometimes referred to as the 'zombie walk' by frequent hikers due to the fact that you need to begin and end on this trail to reach many others to do summits. At the end of long hikes, like the Bonds, walking out late at night is like being a tired zombie!"

Chapter 10

MORE TO KNOW BEFORE YOU GO

I n this section, I've compiled some information that will be of interest and/or help when planning a visit to the Kancamagus Highway, depending on the length of time you may spend in the area. Some of this information is weather-related, while other information is categorized by the various types of activities that can be experienced in this area of the White Mountain National Forest (WMNF). I've also included some of the pertinent rules, regulations and best practices advice from the U.S. Forest Service that relate to the sites and activities discussed above. However, this section is not exhaustive, and rules and laws are always subject to change, so if in doubt, it is always best to check out their website, https://www. fs.usda.gov/detail/whitemountain, or contact the WMNF office directly (603 536 6100).

ON THE HIGHWAY

Except for the first miles at either end in Conway and Lincoln, there are no services along the highway. This means there are no gas or charging stations, or restaurants or food services, for some thirty-two miles.

There are only several public restroom facilities after you leave the Saco River Ranger Station, as detailed in chapter 6. Except for those at the Russell-Colbath House, most are not fully accessible to people with disabilities.

Early tourist map of the
Kancamagus Highway,
seen at the center.
*Courtesy White Mountain
Attractions Association.*

Cell phone service along the Kanc once out of Conway and Lincoln, as of this writing, is virtually nonexistent, meaning you will have no bars. At this point, your cell phone is most useful as a camera, rather than as an instant communication device. Of course, these limitations are part of the challenge, and the fun, of getting back to nature.

Be a good steward to the land no matter your activity, whether hiking or visiting developed sites and overlooks. In the last few years, sadly, some areas have been badly treated by a minority of visitors who leave trash and other waste in their wake. Several of the scenic sites along the Kanc do have trash receptacles, but if some don't, consider them carry in, carry out places when it comes to refuse, and please do your part and take home with you what you brought.

Weather conditions can vary and change quickly along the Kancamagus Highway, especially in the spring and late fall/early winter seasons. When snow is on the ground, be aware that even if the day is clear and sunny, at higher elevations snow can be blown across the road, resulting in some slippery conditions.

When snowy conditions exist, the most common question asked of the Forest Service is whether the highway is open. The Kancamagus Highway is in fact a year-round highway that never closes. However, during or just after heavy snow or other storm situations, the highway may not be fully plowed (as is common of many secondary state roads) or cleared. Use common sense in these situations, and check local weather reports in advance.

Drivers on the Kanc at night, especially in the fall, should exercise great care while traveling. Dozens of moose and deer collisions happen every year in northern New Hampshire, sometimes with fatal consequences.

Any vehicle can drive this highway, though the section through Kancamagus Pass does have some steeper grades. If your vehicle is in good operating condition, the drive is not difficult for modern-make vehicles. However, older cars that have smaller engines without fuel injection will labor to make their way up—but even in this case, you'll make it soon enough, just like the cars built in the 1930s and 1940s that were the first to travel the highway.

WILDLIFE

If you're heading out to potential wildlife viewing spots, be sure to bring what you'll need in addition to photographic and viewing equipment, including a chair, mosquito repellant, water and food. No matter where you go to do your viewing, peace and quiet is essential, as wildlife will not usually make an appearance if noisy humans are about. It is often the case that the wait will be longer than you expect, and though there are no guarantees, hopefully your patience and efforts will be rewarded.

Never feed wild animals, as over time this can make them dependent on humans.

Never interfere with a baby animal while out in the wild. Whether it's a bear cub, baby bird or a fawn you encounter, good intentions can lead to bad results. Instead, it is best to leave them alone where they are, and should you think they might be injured, place a call to New Hampshire Fish and Game so that they can check out the situation. Remember, it is against the law to bring baby animals home with you.

Should you encounter a moose in person, whether it be along the highway or on a hiking trail, use caution. Moose are not known generally to attack humans, but they can be ornery during mating season or if a calf is in the area. Do not approach them at a close distance or harass them in any way. If a moose is blocking your path on a hiking trail, stop and wait until it has moved on, rather than bushwhacking around it and making noise. Some people are tempted to approach moose to get a close-up photo, but this is extremely ill-advised. Instead, enjoy the encounter from a safe distance, and let your telephoto camera lens do the work.

If you encounter a bear in your campsite or along a hiking trail, stay calm and do not run away. Instead, back away slowly. Loud noises will often scare them away.

For birders hoping to see rare examples during their visit, check out the frequent updates available on the New Hampshire Audubon website at https://www.nhaudubon.org/education/birds-and-birding/rare-bird-alerts/.

For those with an interest in natural history, I highly recommend the book *At the North of Bearcamp Water* by Frank Bolles. Published in 1893, it is a beautifully written and classic early account of the birds and other wildlife to be found in the area of the southern White Mountains.

FISHING

For those who plan to go fishing during your visit to the Kanc, a license is required and can be obtained online through New Hampshire Fish and Game at https://www.wildlife.state.nh.us/licensing/.

For most bodies of water, including the Swift River, state regulations as of this writing allow for five fish or five pounds, whichever is reached first, on a daily basis, with the season running from January 1 to October 15. Several ponds—Greely, Falls and the Sawyer Ponds—are remote ponds that do not allow motors, but as of this time there are no other restrictions. For the most up-to-date information, go to https://www.eregulations.com/newhampshire/freshwater.

CAMPING

It is important that campers know the rules laid out by the Forest Service for these White Mountain sites. The most up-to-date information and camping rates may be found at https://www.fs.usda.gov/activity/whitemountain/recreation/camping-cabins.

As of this writing, all reservations, if allowed, must be made by going online at https://www.recreation.gov/ or by calling 877 444 6777, the National Recreation Reservation Service. Please do not call the Forest Service or local ranger stations directly, as they cannot make reservations. The Forest Service also emphasizes that any reservations must be made at least seven days in advance and that those campgrounds listed as first-come, first-served" sites are just that. There are no waiting lists to which you can have your name added. Some of the campgrounds offer a combination of bookings, with some first-come, first-served sites and others that can be reserved in advance.

The payment for WMNF camping sites is simple: place the cash for your stay (rates are clearly posted) inside the envelopes provided at the self-serve pay kiosk, and deposit the envelope in the box at each site (sometimes nicknamed "iron rangers"). These boxes are closely monitored by the hosts, so don't forget; otherwise your campsite may be paid a visit by the host seeking payment.

Each individual site is limited to eight persons, unless otherwise stated, and two vehicles, with an additional charge for the second vehicle. Most have a picnic table and a fire ring. There are no electrical hookups.

The White Mountain National Forest follows strict rules in regard to camp firewood. If coming from outside of New Hampshire or Maine, you cannot bring in firewood from out of state unless this wood is clearly labeled and certified heat-treated. Because such importation of non-treated wood in the past has led to forest infestations from various insect pests, laws were passed making it illegal to bring in this commodity from out of state or Canada. Campground officials and rangers do take note of what's coming in and out and will issue violations, which can result in hefty fines and a loss of your firewood. If you're coming from out of state, there are many places along the way in New Hampshire that offer local or treated firewood for sale, and camp firewood is usually sold by the hosts on-site.

All campgrounds, unless otherwise noted, are in operation from Memorial Day to Columbus Day, the Hancock Campground and Radeke Cabin being the only exceptions.

For a map of each of the campgrounds listed in chapter 8, please check at https://www.fs.usda.gov/Internet/FSE_DOCUMENTS/stelprdb5372642.pdf. Dogs are allowed at White Mountain National Forest campsites, but they must be kept on a leash in developed areas, and owners are responsible for picking up their waste.

It is important also to note that, unlike some other campgrounds in the state, those on the Kancamagus Highway are remote, and none of these sites has a camp store like many private campgrounds do, so plan ahead. Should you run out of anything, a run to a store in Lincoln or Conway could mean as much as a thirty-mile round trip.

All WMNF campgrounds have hosts on-site who are there to help campers, and they have a general reputation for friendliness. However, the rules for the campgrounds, especially noise levels after hours, are enforced so as to keep the White Mountain camping experience a family-friendly one.

It is generally true that the smaller campgrounds on the Kanc are less noisy in nature than the larger ones like Jigger Johnson, so if it's peace and quiet you truly seek, campgrounds like Passaconaway and Big Rock may be more to your liking.

Campers should keep campsites clean and keep all food safely stored when not in use. There are plenty of bears in the White Mountains, and if you are careless in this regard, they'll know it. They can pick up a scent sometimes from as much as a mile away! Some campsites offer bear boxes for this purpose, but most do not. Bears are agile climbers; food secured in a tree must be hung at least ten feet off the ground and at least four feet away from the trunk of the tree, using a strong rope and making sure the branch to which it is secured is also strong. Leaving open food containers in your vehicle can even be a potential problem. Bears may get wind of this and have been known, if the car window is rolled down even a fraction, to break it to gain access inside.

Hiking

Hikers who are new to the White Mountains should be aware that weather conditions here, even in the summer, can change drastically and vary greatly. On a Kancamagus trailhead in July, you may begin a hike at, say 70 degrees Fahrenheit, but depending on the elevation of your chosen trail and the time of day, that temperature could easily drop twenty or thirty degrees or even more as you go along.

There is no reliable cell phone service on trails or most anywhere along the Kancamagus Highway.

Hikers should know that removing any historic artifacts, such as old cans and bottles, found along WMNF trails to take home as a historic souvenir not only disturbs the archaeology of the area but is also against the law.

Hikers, whether new or experienced, should always follow the "take-in-take-out" ethos and leave nothing of their presence behind them. Leave the trails and woods as you found them, and please help preserve the trails and the White Mountains for those who will follow!

All hikers are advised to purchase a Hike Safe card. This can be done through the New Hampshire Fish and Game website at https://www. nhfishandgame.com/. This card, whether for an individual or family, currently costs just twenty-five dollars per individual or thirty-five dollars per family and is good for one year in New Hampshire only. In effect, it provides hiking insurance, protecting the holder from paying rescue costs should they be injured or experience an incident that requires a search and rescue mission. Even the simplest of rescues, of which there are about sixty a year in the White Mountains, can cost thousands or even tens of thousands of dollars, especially if a helicopter is involved. This card covers these costs, provided that the hiker was not acting negligently and had the proper gear along or was not acting in such a way as to create the emergency. Note that if you hold a New Hampshire fishing or hunting license, you already have this protection.

Dogs are allowed on hiking trails in the White Mountain National Forest, but owners should pick up after them, and they must be kept on a leash when at the trailhead or any developed areas. Owners should also be sure that their pet is up for the planned hike. Should your dog have an emergency, New Hampshire Fish and Game does not perform rescue missions for pets. However, the hiking community is a friendly one, and it has been the case many times over the years that other hikers have stopped to assist a pet in need on New Hampshire trails and helped an owner in carrying an injured canine back down a trail.

Hikers should know the route they are taking and what to expect, be familiar with the expected weather forecast and have the proper gear along. This includes the proper footwear (tennis shoes won't do), rain gear, warm clothes and accessories for all possible conditions (a T-shirt won't cut it in White Mountain elevations), water (more than you think you might need) and nutrient-dense foods, as well as such necessities as mosquito repellant, a first-aid kit, a map, matches and a lighter, a flashlight or headlamp, a whistle (in case you get lost) and a pocket knife. A compass is an absolute must. Though GPS units will also be of great help, reception is not always reliable, so these should not be your sole directional aid. Be sure to leave information about your plans, including your departure time and expected return time, with family or friends.

PHOTOGRAPHY

Depending on how much time you plan on spending along the Kanc, and what stops you may make, with a little planning and forethought, you will be able to capture some photographic memories that you will cherish for years to come. To that end, it is important to have the right equipment along, but this does not mean you have to spend a fortune. Whether you have a digital camera or plan to use your smartphone, a tripod is a must so that you will have a stable platform from which to shoot. If you're using a smartphone, make sure the tripod you buy has an adapter for its use. You may also want to consider using a wireless remote shutter for your smartphone. Bluetooth units can be easily purchased for under ten dollars.

In addition to your photo devices, a set of binoculars are a must, especially for birders. There are also available cell phone adapter mounts for binoculars. Though they take some practice to learn how to use, these adapters are pretty handy, showing on your camera screen what is visible through the binoculars. Mounting the binoculars with this adapter on a tripod is the best way to go, as without it, the tremor will be too great, and your photos will be of poor quality, if captured at all.

Drone or unmanned aircraft photography along the Kancamagus Highway was once allowed but as of 2019 has been prohibited. Drones cannot be landed within a quarter of a mile of any trailhead or developed scenic site, any campground, the Kancamagus Highway itself, Bear Notch Road and Passaconaway/Dugway Road. Furthermore, they may not be landed within a quarter of a mile of the Champney Falls Trail, Champney and Sabbaday Falls, East and Greely Ponds and Loon Mountain. This is not a complete listing of all restricted areas. Though this information is sometimes posted at various sites along the Kanc, visitors are responsible for knowing the laws regarding drone use. Note that the aerial photographs of the Kanc shown in this book were taken prior to the time these restrictions went into effect.

Other Recreational Opportunities

Whitewater kayaking is very popular on the Swift River in the early spring as the river runs high due to the spring melt-off. Though the river is very narrow, seldom more than fifty feet wide, it can be challenging to even experienced boaters due to its rocky nature. There are three major put-in locations to begin (or continue) your trip. The Upper Swift runs four miles from Bear Notch Road to Rocky Gorge and is noted for its flat paddling and beautiful scenery, the Kanc not being too far away but well out of sight and hearing. Class 2 rapids are experienced at first, but these turn into a continuous set of Class 3 rapids as you reach Rocky Gorge. However, going through the gorge itself is not advised, and those unfamiliar with the river will have to scout closely for a suitable take-out, or you may end up going through Rocky Gorge, with serious injury a real possibility. Below Rocky Gorge, you can put in just downstream from the footbridge for the Middle Swift run, but beware, as the riverbank is very steep here. The run in this 2.6-mile area above Lower Falls is mostly Class 3, the most difficult area being the Triple Drop, a section that has several three-foot drops in close proximity. This can be dangerous in times of low water. It is advisable to scout your take-out above Lower Falls before you make your trip, or scout Lower Falls itself if you plan on tackling it. Finally, for the Lower Swift, you can put in in the pool just below the Lower Falls area. If you park here, a parking pass will be required. From here, the river runs just over five miles, dropping in elevation some 377 feet. The first rapid is a Class 4, but thereafter things get easier; the river is rated Class 1–2 for just under two miles. The Swift then becomes more difficult heading downstream, going through Cabin Gorge and the Staircase before continuing on through some Class 3–4 rapids. The take-out here is near the sign for Loon Mountain. Older sources list the sign for the Darby Field Inn as the take-out point, but this sign is no longer present, as the inn is no longer in business. Some of the difficult areas on the Swift River may have to be more closely scouted depending on your experience, though many can be boat scouted. For more detailed information, the American Whitewater site, https://www.americanwhitewater.org/content/River/view/river-detail/1189/main, is always a good place to start.

The Pemigewasset and C.L. Graham overlooks are also a popular destination for amateur stargazers. If you plan to spend a night or two in the area, be sure to bring your telescope and return to these spots after darkness has fallen. Light pollution levels, while not entirely absent, are fairly low here, measuring about a 2 on the Bortle scale, so opportunities for a view of the Milky Way and some great night sky pictures are there for the taking if the weather cooperates.

If you either live nearby or are planning a visit or a stay in the area during the holiday season, did you know that you can cut your very own Christmas tree along the Kancamagus Highway? In fact, the White Mountain National Forest allows a family to cut one tree for this purpose with the purchase of a permit, which costs a mere five dollars as of this writing. While this low price is a real bargain, the experience of cutting one's own handpicked tree is priceless and is a family tradition for many in the area. There are rules, however, that must be followed. The tree can only be cut by hand tools;

Whitewater kayaker on the lower Swift River. The Kancamagus Highway is visible at upper right. *Courtesy Daniel Brasuell.*

A view of the Milky Way from Rocky Gorge. *Jim Lozouski, Shutterstock.com.*

no chainsaws are allowed. Trees cannot be harvested within one hundred feet of the highway, in or near campgrounds or picnic areas or within the Pemigewasset Wilderness. There are also several areas along the Kanc, especially around Lower Falls and Rocky Gorge, where signs are typically posted prohibiting tree cutting. For a current list of guidelines, please check out the WMNF website at https://www.fs.usda.gov/Internet/FSE_DOCUMENTS/stelprdb5277607.pdf.

Hunting is allowed on all WMNF lands within the boundaries of New Hampshire Fish and Game Department laws. A hunting license is required, and there are regulations regarding such activity around the developed recreation sites and ponds along the Kanc. Check out the WMNF website, https://www.fs.usda.gov/activity/whitemountain/recreation/hunting, for the most up-to-date information. Hunters will be required to purchase a pass when parking at some areas along the highway.

Source Bibliography and Further Reading

Ballard, Lisa Densmore. "In the Zone: Exploring the Ecozones of the White Mountains." Appalachian Mountain Club, April 22, 2015. https://www.outdoors.org/resources/amc-outdoors/conservation-and-climate/in-the-zone/.

Beals, Charles Edward Jr. *Passaconaway in the White Mountains*. Boston: Richard G. Badger, 1916. https://books.google.com/books?id=dHAjA QAAMAAJ&printsec=frontcover&source=gbs_ge_summary_r&cad=0# v=onepage&q&f=false.

Belcher, C. Francis. *Logging Railroads of the White Mountains*. Boston: AMC, 1980.

Boisvert, Richard A. "Paleoindian Occupation of the White Mountains, New Hampshire." *Géographie physique et Quaternaire* 53, no. 1 (1999): 1–16. https://www.erudit.org/documentation/rapport/annx3.pdf.

Bolles, Frank. *At the North of Bearcamp Water*. Boston: Houghton Mifflin, 1917. First published 1893.

DeLorme Mapping Company. *The New Hampshire Atlas*. Freeport, ME: DeLorme Mapping, 1988.

Eckstorm, Fannie Hardy. "Who Was Paugus?" *New England Quarterly* 12, no. 2 (1939): 203–26. https://doi.org/10.2307/360412.

Gengras, Justine B., and David Ruel. "National Register of Historic Places Inventory—Nomination Form: Russell/Colbath House." Tilton, NH, October 29, 1986. https://npgallery.nps.gov/NRHP/GetAsset/ NRHP/86003416_text.

Gove, Bill. *Logging Railroads of New Hampshire's North Country*. Littleton, NH: Bondcliff Books, 2009.

Hallamore, Warren S. "The Kancamagus Highway Story." Conway, NH: n.p., 1960. This is a paper read to the Conway Historical Society; the only known copy is held by the New Hampshire Historical Society.

Holbrook, Stewart. *Holy Old Mackinaw: A Natural History of the American Lumberjack*. New York: Macmillan, 1938.

Kimball, Sarah, et. al. "Swift River Corridor Management Plan." Swift River Management Advisory Committee, New Hampshire Department of Environmental Services, May 1994.

Kwasnik, Greg. "Who's the Walking Boss?" *Loon Magazine* (Winter 2016–17), 12–17. https://issuu.com/loonmagazine/docs/loonmag1617_web.

Laskin, Josh. "Greens Cliff: New Hampshire's Mega Backcountry Destination." *Outside*, September 10, 2019. https://www.climbing.com/places/greens-cliff-new-hampshires-mega-backcountry-destination/.

Lawson, Russell M. *Passaconaway's Realm*. Hanover, NH: University Press of New England, 2002.

Lepionka, Mary Ellen. "Chocorua Redux: Revisionist History of a Name." N.d. https://static1.squarespace.com/static/5c6c20254d8711284e8b9a6b/t/5d0bee26d7c9fe00010ea0ac/1561062950571/Chocorua+Redux.pdf.

Merrill, Georgia Drew, ed. *History of Carroll County*. Somersworth, NH: New Hampshire Publishing, 1971. First published 1889.

Monahan, Robert. "Jigger Johnson." *New Hampshire Profiles* 6, no. 4 (April 1957).

———. Robert Monahan Papers, Special—Senate '61—Kancamagus Highway, 1957–1964, MS-1088: Folder 34, Box 22, Rauner Special Collections Library, Dartmouth College, Hanover, NH.

New Hampshire Fish and Game. "Wild Life in New Hampshire," https://www.wildlife.state.nh.us/wildlife/.

Osborne, Keith. "The Kancamagus Highway: A Historical Look at the Development of the Kancamagus Highway." Plymouth, NH: n.p., 1999. This is a paper prepared by the author for the Social Science Department at Plymouth State College and is the first scholarly work regarding the highway.

Ouellette, Randy. "Fly Fishing the Swift River—Complete Guide to This Beautiful NH River." Hiking & Fishing. https://hikingandfishing.com/fly-fishing-swift-river-nh/.

Russack, Rick, et al. "White Mountain History." WhiteMountainHistory.org. https://whitemountainhistory.org/About_Us.html. This excellent website contains many great local history articles and images.

Smith, Steven D. *Ponds & Lakes of the White Mountains*, Woodstock, VT: Backcountry Publications, 1993.

Smith, Steven D., and Mike Dickerman, eds. *Appalachian Mountain Club White Mountain Guide*. Boston: AMC, 2012.

State of New Hampshire Department of Environmental Services. "Environmental Fact Sheet—The Swift River," WD-R&L-12, May 2019.

Sweetser, Moses, ed. *The White Mountains: A Handbook for Travelers*. 3rd ed. Boston: James R. Osgood, 1880. https://books.google.com/books?id=y fsaAAAAYAAJ&printsec=frontcover&source=gbs_ge_summary_r&cad= 0#v=onepage&q&f=false.

Tekiela, Stan. *Birds of New Hampshire & Vermont*. Cambridge, MN: Adventure Publications, 2016.

Walker, Joseph B. *Our New Hampshire Forests—An Address* [...]. Concord, NH: Ira C. Evans, 1891. Available online at https://books.google.com/books ?id=CygDAAAAYAAJ&printsec=frontcover&source=gbs_ge_summary_ r&cad=0#v=onepage&q&f=false.

White Mountain National Forest. "The Russell Colbath House." N.d. https:// www.wmiaofnh.org/uploads/1/1/2/4/11241524/colbathhandout.pdf.